SEATTLE
celebrated
chefs

A special partnership featuring the area's
best restaurants in support of local non-profit
organizations.

www.celebratedchefs.com

Recipes From the Premier Chefs in Our Community

The Celebrated Chefs cookbook is your insider's guide to a collection of tantalizing recipes from the finest restaurants in the Greater Seattle area. Each chef has provided a signature dish for you to try at home as a sneak peak to what lies in store when you walk through the door. The restaurants featured in this limited edition cookbook are recognized for their dedication to delicious food, quality ingredients and outstanding service, but their commitment doesn't stop there...

A Great Fundraiser for Your Organization

Celebrated Chefs restaurants donate up to 5% of your bill to your nonprofit organization each and every time you dine. It's simple and it's free - just pay your bill using the same credit card you enrolled, and the restaurant donation to your designated cause occurs automatically. Whether for business or pleasure, the more you dine, the more funds you help raise.

Make a point to frequent these exceptional restaurants. They are proud to support your organization, and we hope you will support them through your ongoing patronage.
Thank you from all of us at Celebrated Chefs.
Visit us anytime at www.celebratedchefs.com for the latest information on the program.

Bon Appétit

KING
SALMON
$ 7.⁹⁹/lb

· 5

EVERY TIME YOU DINE, A DONATION IS MADE TO YOUR GROUP!

PURPLE CAFÉ & WINE BAR *pg 26*
www.thepurplecafe.com

1225 Fourth Avenue
Seattle WA 98101
(206) 829-2280

430 106th Avenue NE
Bellevue WA 98004
(425) 502-6292

323 Park Place Center
Kirkland WA 98033
(425) 828-3772

14459 Woodinville-Redmond Rd NE
Woodinville WA 98072
(425) 483-7129

QUEEN CITY GRILL *pg 194*
2201 First Avenue
Seattle WA 98121
(206) 443-0975
www.queencitygrill.com

RAY'S BOATHOUSE *pg 88*
6049 Seaview Avenue NW
Seattle WA 98107
(206) 789-3770
www.rays.com

RISTORANTE ITALIANISSIMO *pg 164*
15608 NE Woodinville-Duvall PL
Woodinville WA 98072
(425) 485-6888
www.italianissimoristorante.com

ROVER'S *pg 16*
2808 E Madison Street
Seattle WA 98112
(206) 325-7442
www.thechefinthehat.com

RUSSELL'S *pg 106*
3305 Monte Villa Parkway
Bothell WA 98021
(425) 486-4072
www.rdlcatering.com

RUTH'S CHRIS STEAK HOUSE *pg 84*
www.ruthschris.com

565 Bellevue Square
Bellevue WA 98004
(425) 451-1550

727 Pine Street
Seattle WA 98101
(206) 624-8524

SALISH LODGE & SPA *pg 98*
6501 Railroad Avenue
Snoqualmie WA 98065
(425) 888-2556
www.salishlodge.com

SAZERAC *pg 162*
1101 Fourth Avenue
Seattle WA 98101
(206) 624-7755
www.sazeracrestaurant.com

SEASTAR *pg 14*
www.seastarrestaurant.com

1101 Fourth Avenue
Seattle WA 98101
(206) 462-4364

205 108th Avenue NE
Bellevue WA 98004
(425) 456-0010

SHUCKERS *pg 60*
411 University Street
Seattle WA 98101
(206) 621-1984
www.fairmont.com/seattle

SIX SEVEN *pg 132*
2411 Alaskan Way, Pier 67
Seattle WA 98121
(206) 269-4575
www.edgewaterhotel.com

SKYCITY AT THE NEEDLE *pg 104*
400 Broad Street
Seattle WA 98109
(206) 905-2100
www.spaceneedle.com

SPRING HILL *pg 122*
4437 California Avenue SW
Seattle WA 98116
(206) 935-1075
www.springhillnorthwest.com

SPUR GASTROPUB *pg 178*
113 Blanchard Street
Seattle WA 98121
(206) 728-6706
www.spurseattle.com

STUMBLING GOAT BISTRO *pg 94*
6722 Greenwood Ave N
Seattle WA 98103
(206) 784-3535
www.stumblinggoatbistro.com

TASTE *pg 80*
1300 First Avenue
Seattle WA 98101
(206) 903-5291
www.tastesam.com

TAVOLÀTA *pg 154*
2323 Second Avenue
Seattle WA 98121
(206) 838-8008
www.ethanstowellrestaurants.com

TEN MERCER *pg 66*
10 Mercer Street
Seattle WA 98109
(206) 691-3723
www.tenmercer.com

THE GEORGIAN *pg 190*
411 University Street
Seattle WA 98101
(206) 621-7889
www.fairmont.com/seattle

THE PIKE PUB & BREWERY *pg 142*
1415 First Avenue
Seattle WA 98101
(206) 622-6044
www.pikebrewing.com

celebrated ▶ make a
chefs reservation now
www.celebratedchefs.com

LET THE DELICIOUS FUN BEGIN

The stage is set with the first bite you place before your guests. Appetizers and starters are designed to awaken the palate with a small plate of something boldly flavored, slightly rich, and maybe just a bit spicy. The beauty of these little dishes is their flexibility. Some are casual, others more upscale.

Some can be dialed down to be finger food for a party while others double as entrees when served in larger portions. All allow chefs to be creative, and, on occasion, whimsical, while their deliciousness builds the diners' anticipation for the remaining courses. Wow your dinner guests by preparing any of the tasty starter recipes featured here and you'll create something that has your guests wondering what will be next.

www.celebratedchefs.com

APPETIZERS & STARTERS

Cafe Juanita

Driven by her passion for the foods of Northern Italy, Chef Holly Smith opened Cafe Juanita in 2000. Her hallmark rests with the special care she takes to cook seasonally with the finest, mainly organic, local produce and artisan products from Italy and the Pacific Northwest. The menu paired with an award-winning wine list and superior service, continues to earn Café Juanita local and national acclaim.

Grilled Asparagus with Duck Egg and Parmigiano Reggiano

Kitchen Note: Chef Smith recommends cooking each of the duck eggs in its own skillet all at the same time. If you have enough skillets, you can do the same, though you can also cook the eggs together in one large skillet.

Serves 4

28 spears asparagus, preferably local harvest
1/4 cup extra virgin olive oil
1/2 cup Plugra or other European style unsalted butter
4 duck eggs or chicken eggs, preferably organic
Kosher salt and freshly ground black pepper
1/2 cup shaved Parmigiano Reggiano

Preheat an outdoor grill. Toss the asparagus spears in the olive oil and grill the asparagus until nicely browned and just tender, 3 to 4 minutes.

Melt the butter in a large skillet, preferably nonstick, over medium heat. Carefully crack the eggs into the skillet, as well separated from one another as possible. Season the eggs lightly with salt and pepper. Baste the yolks with some of the melted butter as they cook. When the white is nearly fully cooked, after 3 or 4 minutes, take the pan from the heat and let sit for a minute or two.

Arrange the grilled asparagus on individual plates , fanning them out slightly. Top the asparagus with the fried duck eggs, leaving the asparagus tips exposed. Spoon some of the butter from the skillet over the eggs. Top with shavings of Parmigiano Reggiano and serve right away.

serve your community while being served at Cafe Juanita!

visit www.celebratedchefs.com
www.cafejuanita.com

Chef Holly Smith

Executive Chef and Owner Holly Smith is the *2008 James Beard Foundation* winner for *Best Chef Northwest* and has been recognized in countless publications including *Gourmet, Robb Report, Wine Spectator,* as well as a 2009 nomination for *Best Restaurant Service* by the *James Beard Foundation.* Originally from Maryland, Chef Smith earned her culinary degree and later moved to Seattle and cooked in many notable kitchens before opening Cafe Juanita in 2000.

seastar

Seastar Restaurant and Raw Bar features an inspired seafood-centered menu with local Pacific Northwest favorites and seasonal preparations. The upbeat Raw Bar offers sushi, sashimi, ceviche, poke, oysters, and shellfish, or enjoy the comfort of the luxurious Seastar dining room. Either way, Seastar's talented staff will make you feel right at home.

Cedar Plank Roasted Wild Mushrooms

Kitchen Note: For this recipe you can find cedar planks and Chef Howie's own brand of porcini mushroom rub at Seastar restaurants and online at www.plankcooking.com. At Seastar each diner's serving is prepared on a personal plank, but you can cook enough for two servings on one large plank when replicating this at home. If you are unable to get your hands on a jar of Chef Howie's rub, you can use other seasoning rubs that include dried mushrooms or your favorite rub or salt. You can also substitute other seasonal or wild mushrooms for those listed here. These mushrooms make a delicious side dish as well, enough to serve four.

Serves 2 to 4

8 ounces portobello mushroom caps, cut into 1 1/2 by 2 inch chunks
8 ounces cremini or white button mushrooms, trimmed and halved
4 ounces shiitake mushrooms, stem trimmed and cut into 2 inch pieces
6 tablespoons olive oil
2 tablespoons freshly squeezed lemon juice
1 tablespoon porcini mushroom rub
1 teaspoon minced garlic
1 teaspoon finely chopped fresh thyme
1/4 teaspoon finely chopped fresh rosemary
1/4 teaspoon finely chopped fresh sage
Salt and freshly ground black pepper
Herb sprigs, for garnish
Lemon slices, for garnish

Preheat the oven to 375°F.

Combine the mushrooms in a large bowl and add the olive oil, lemon juice, mushroom rub, garlic, thyme, rosemary, and sage with a good pinch each of salt and pepper. Toss well to evenly coat the mushrooms with the seasonings.

Arrange the mushrooms in an even layer on a cedar plank, not quite to the edge. Roast the mushrooms until tender and lightly browned around the edges, 12 to 15 minutes. Serve the mushrooms directly from the plank at the table, or arrange on individual plates before serving. Garnish with a few herb sprigs and lemon slices.

serve your community while being served at seastar!

visit www.celebratedchefs.com
www.seastarrestaurant.com

Chef John Howie

John Howie began his culinary career at age 15 and his training ground was many of Seattle's finest restaurants. As opening chef at Palisade in 1992 and during his ten-year tenure, the restaurant became the premier special occasion dining spot. In 2002, John opened the first of four award-winning restaurants, Seastar in Bellevue and in 2009, Seastar in Seattle. This restaurant is a culmination of his dream to showcase the best of the Pacific Northwest and has received critical acclaim on both the local and national stage.

Rover's

On a visit to Seattle in 1987, Chef Thierry Rautureau came across a restaurant for sale called Rover's. Today this intimate little restaurant in Madison Valley is filled with art and warm sophistication - a trademark of the friendly French chef, known as the "Chef in the Hat"!!! In its 21 years, Rover's has won both local and national awards for cuisine, service, and wine list.

Halibut Ceviche with Mango and Cucumber

Kitchen Note: Serve with a small salad of mesclun greens alongside

Serves 6 to 8

1 pound halibut fillet, skin and pin bones removed
1/2 cup freshly squeezed lime juice
1/4 cup seasoned rice vinegar
2 tablespoons olive oil
4 cloves garlic, lightly crushed
1 small red onion, thinly sliced
1 mango, peeled, seeded, and finely diced
1 English cucumber, finely diced
1 small Jalapeño, cored, seeded, and finely minced
  (more or less, to your taste)
1 teaspoon finely chopped lemon balm or cilantro
Sea salt and freshly ground white pepper

Cut the halibut into 1/2 inch cubes or thin strips about 1/4 inch wide and put them in a nonreactive bowl. Stir together the lime juice, vinegar, olive oil, and garlic in a small bowl, then pour this over the halibut and stir gently to mix. Cover the bowl with plastic wrap and refrigerate for 1 to 2 hours, stirring once or twice.

About 30 minutes before serving, stir the red onion, mango, cucumber, jalapeño, and cilantro into the ceviche. Season lightly with salt and pepper, toss gently, and refrigerate until ready to serve.

Taste the ceviche for seasoning, adding more salt or pepper if needed. Discard the crushed garlic cloves. Spoon the ceviche into martini glasses or small glass dishes and serve.

serve your community while being
served at Rover's!

visit www.celebratedchefs.com
www.thechefinthehat.com

Chef Thierry Rautureau

Chef and Owner Thierry Rautureau is passionate about his commitment to food as art. Born in the Muscadet region of France, Chef Rautureau began his cooking apprenticeship in Anjou, France at the age of 14. At 20, he took his professional experience to La Fontaine in Chicago and a number of other top restaurants, before purchasing and opening Rover's in 1987. Chef Rautureau won the *James Beard Foundation Award* for *Best Chef Northwest* in 1998.

ART Restaurant

ART Restaurant celebrates authentic Pacific Northwest cuisine with unique global influences. ART provides exquisite views of Elliott Bay through floor to ceiling windows from: the main dining room, the perfect spot for a business lunch or dinner with friends; ART Lounge, the city's hottest spot for happy hour and inventive cocktails; the private dining room, an intimate dining experience and The Counter, unlimited cheese and tapas tables set in front of the 12-foot wine wall.

Crisp Horseradish Crusted Oysters

Kitchen Note: Fresh horseradish makes all the difference here and a microplane grater will work best to create fine shavings that blend well in the bread crumb coating. Jarred horseradish is a bit too wet for this use. Look for fresh horseradish in the produce section near other specialty products.

Serves 4

2 eggs
1 cup fresh bread crumbs or dried panko crumbs
1 tablespoons freshly grated horseradish
24 medium oysters, shucked, bottom shells cleaned
   and reserved for presentation
1 cup canola oil, for frying
2 cups rock salt, for presentation

Celery Root and Apple Slaw

1 cup grated celery root
1 cup grated apple (Granny Smith or Fuji)
1/4 cup grated carrot
1/4 cup grated yellow onion
1/4 cup mayonnaise
1 tablespoon chopped flat-leaf parsley
2 teaspoon freshly squeezed lemon juice
Salt and freshly ground black pepper

For the slaw, combine the celery root, apple, carrot, onion, mayonnaise, parsley, and lemon juice in a medium bowl and toss well to mix. Season to taste with salt and pepper. Refrigerate for 1 to 2 hours before serving.

Put the eggs in a medium bowl and beat well. In another medium bowl, combine the bread crumbs and horseradish and stir well to evenly mix. Working with 4 to 5 oysters at a time, dip them first in the egg mixture, then lift out and allow excess egg to drip off. Add the oysters to the bread crumb mixture and toss to evenly coat. Set aside on a plate and repeat with the remaining oysters.

Before cooking the oysters, cover the base of 4 serving plates with the rock salt and nestle the bottom oyster shells into the salt, 6 per plate.

Heat the oil in a large skillet, preferably nonstick, over medium heat. Add a pinch of the remaining breadcrumb mixture to the pan. If it browns in a few seconds, the pan is too hot; reduce the heat a bit. The crumbs should brown in 30 to 45 seconds. Add half of the oysters to the skillet and brown well on both sides, about 2 minutes total. Transfer to paper towels to drain while cooking the remaining oysters.

Spoon some of the celery root and apple slaw into each oyster shell, top with a crisp oyster, and serve right away.

serve your community while being served at ART Restaurant!

visit www.celebratedchefs.com
www.artrestaurantseattle.com

Chef Kerry Sear

Executive Chef Kerry Sear retuned to Four Seasons in 2008 after a decade as chef/owner of Cascadia. "I like to infuse all my food with a bit of joie de vivre. Food should be not only elegant and delicious, but also memorable in a way that makes you want to return for more," says Chef Sear. He consistently combines high-quality ingredients from the Pike Place Market, offering ART guests a seasonal menu with global influences.

Matt's in the Market

Many say that the Pike Place Market is the heart of Seattle, leaving Matt's in the Market at its center. Matt's offers spectacular views of Elliott Bay, the Olympics and the Market's famed clock through the charming arched windows. Celebrating community, local sustainability, and seasonality, Chef Gerl creates an inspired menu, highlighting market fresh ingredients provided by our Pacific Northwest farmers, foragers, fishermen and winemakers.

Spot Prawns With Cotija Grits and Guajillo Chile-Honey Citronette

Kitchen Note: Spot prawns can typically be found fresh in the Northwest in May and June as well as October and November. Some seafood markets may have them frozen to be available the rest of the year. Guajillo chiles are a moderately spicy dried chile; if you're unable to find them, you can use New Mexican chiles though they tend to be milder in flavor.

Serves 6
1 tablespoon olive oil
18 fresh spot prawns
Cilantro sprigs, for garnish

Citronette Dressing

2 Guajillo chiles, stemmed, seeded, and thinly sliced
1/4 cup honey
1/4 cup freshly squeezed lime juice
2 cloves garlic, slivered
1/2 cup canola oil

Cotija Grits

2 cups water
1 cup whipping cream
1 cup quick-cooking grits (preferably Albers brand)
2 tablespoons grated or crumbled Cotija cheese
Kosher salt

For the grits, combine the water and cream in a medium saucepan and bring just to a boil over medium-high heat. Gradually add the grits, whisking constantly, and cook until the grits are tender and the mixture has thickened, 6 to 8 minutes. Whisk in the Cotija cheese and season to taste with salt. Keep warm over low heat.

For the citronette, combine the chiles, honey, and lime juice in a small saucepan and warm over medium-low heat until the chiles are soft, 5 to 10 minutes. Add the garlic and take the pan from the heat. Whisk in the oil with salt to taste.

For the prawns, heat the olive oil in a large skillet over medium-high heat. Add the spot prawns and cook just until opaque through, 1 to 2 minutes per side.

Spoon the warm grits into individual plates and top with the spot prawns. Drizzle the citronette over, garnish with cilantro, and serve.

serve your community while being served at Matt's in the Market!
visit www.celebratedchefs.com
www.mattsinthemarket.com

Chef Chester Gerl

Executive Chef Chester Gerl attended Western Culinary in Portland, studying under chef and master gardener Dan Brophy. Prior to joining Matt's in the Market, Gerl spent four years as Executive Chef at Place Pigalle and also worked under famed Chef Tamara Murphy at Brasa. His travels to Thailand, Vietnam, the Caribbean, Spain and Mexico (where he studied under Rick Bayless) has been paramount in defining his culinary approach.

Urbane

Housed in the LEED-certified Olive 8 tower, Urbane's commitment to sustainability is illustrated by the decision to feature local ingredients. By sourcing our raw materials locally, we are actively engaged in reducing Urbane's impact on the planet, while presenting an approachable farm-to-table menu. Wood and stone décor elements emphasize Urbane's connection to nature, while soaring windows and the vibrant cityscape complement the experience.

Herbal Dungeness Crab Cakes

Kitchen Note: The rich crab cakes with tart-sweet tomato chutney are often served with a fresh, bright salad of fennel and watercress alongside, with a simple dressing of olive oil and lemon juice. You'll have more tomato chutney than is needed here, but extra will keep for a week or two in the refrigerator. It will be great with roasted pork, grilled salmon, and other simply prepared dishes.

Serves 6

1 pound Dungeness crab meat
1/3 cup dried bread crumbs
1/4 cup coarsely chopped fresh chives
1/4 cup coarsely chopped fresh basil
2 tablespoons coarsely chopped fresh flat-leaf
  parsley leaves
1 egg yolk
1 tablespoon mayonnaise, more if needed
1/2 teaspoon Worcestershire sauce
1/2 teaspoon Sriracha or other hot chile sauce

Coating

1/2 cup all-purpose flour
1 cup fresh or dried bread crumbs
2 eggs, beaten

Tomato Chutney

1/2 cup chopped onion
8 cloves garlic
2 tablespoons olive oil
1/2 teaspoon yellow mustard seeds
1/2 teaspoon cumin seeds
1/2 teaspoon fennel seeds

3 cup diced tomatoes
  (drained canned tomatoes work well)
3/4 cup red wine vinegar
1/2 cup sugar
1 teaspoon salt
Pinch cayenne

For the chutney, combine the onion and garlic in a mini-processor or food processor and process to finely chop, nearly the consistency of a paste, scraping down the sides a few times.

Heat the oil in a medium saucepan over medium heat. Add the mustard seeds and cook, stirring, until they begin to pop, about 15 seconds. Add cumin and fennel seeds and toast, shaking the pan gently, until aromatic but not too browned, about 30 seconds longer. Add the onion/garlic mixture and cook, stirring, until well blended with the spices and aromatic, 1 to 2 minutes. Stir in the tomatoes, vinegar, sugar, salt, and cayenne. Reduce the heat to medium and simmer until thickened, about 20 minutes. Transfer the chutney to a bowl and let cool. Cover and refrigerate until ready to serve.

continued on page 24

serve your community while being
served at Urbane!

visit www.celebratedchefs.com
www.urbaneseattle.com

Chef Dan Gilmore

A passion for adventure drives Chef de Cuisine Dan Gilmore to constantly experiment with new flavors and techniques. His extensive travels have helped him develop a love of different cultures and a knack for combining flavors in unexpected ways. Raised in Tucson, AZ, Dan has been a Seattle resident for the past seven years and has worked in many of the area's best restaurants. In his kitchen, Chef Gilmore proudly instills his passion and commitment for sustainable food with his staff.

continued from page 23

Pick over the crab meat to remove any bits of shell or cartilage, then squeeze the meat gently in your hands to remove excess water. Put the crab in a medium bowl and add the bread crumbs, chives, basil, parsley, egg yolk, mayonnaise, Worcestershire sauce, and Sriracha. Stir gently to evenly mix. If the mixture seems a bit dry, add another tablespoon or so of mayonnaise; it should hold its shape when pressed into a cake.

Form the crab mixture into 6 compact disks about 2 1/2 inches in diameter. Pressing the mixture into a ring mold is a helpful technique to assure that the mixture remains cohesive.

Put the flour on one plate and the bread crumbs on another. Put the beaten egg in a shallow bowl. Working with 1 crab cake at a time, lightly coat it in the flour, patting to remove excess. Dip both sides of the cake in the beaten egg and lift out, allowing excess to drip off. Finally, coat the cake evenly in the bread crumbs, patting to remove excess. Set aside on a plate while coating the remaining crab cakes.

Heat the oil in a large skillet over medium heat. Brown the crab cakes well, 3 to 4 minutes per side. Arrange the crab cakes on individual plates, add a spoonful of the chutney alongside, and serve.

Cocktail Culture

It seems to have started simply enough, the resurgence of the martini a handful of years ago. We felt elegantly refined, sipping our brightly chilled gin (or vodka, if preferred), with a couple plump olives perched below the surface.

Old-school cocktails continue to make a comeback in a big way. Not just the popular martinis and old-fashioneds and sidecars, but also less-common slings and sours and rickeys. Drinkers can increasingly try out the classics that helped set the stage for the never-ending range of contemporary cocktails that bar masters are whipping up today. Just like in the kitchen, the modern cocktail and the traditional can live happily side-by-side, giving customers even more selections.

What's adding an interesting dimension to today's cocktails is the growth of artisan distillers across the country. While some spirits have distinct traditions that may include strict legal production requirements (such as bourbon), most spirits offer latitude for style and flavor influences that a distiller can bring to the table. In some cases, a distiller can play around nearly as much as a chef!

Take gin, for instance. Aside from the obligatory presence of juniper berries in the mix, the class of gin is wide open to creative input. Distillers can employ different types of stills and different methods for infusing the aromatics into the base of neutral spirit. And those aromatics can include a great range of flavors, including spices, citrus fruits, herbs, even flowers. Just like the chef, the distiller is looking for distinctive flavors that offer a pleasing balance. Their efforts now give those behind the bar dozens of gins to choose from, products that can be used for just the right cocktail! One's great in a martini, another will be better in an aviation, yet another ideal for a gin and tonic.

Back on the scene (after decades of being blacklisted from American bars) is absinthe. The wily wormwood that is famously a traditional ingredient of absinthe has been revealed as likely not the thing that drove people nearly crazy over a century ago. And very little is used in the spirit's recipe anyway, as the foundation also relies on anise and other botanicals. A whole ritual surrounds the drinking of absinthe in the classic fashion, though now it's also embellishing modern cocktails, as mixologists get creative with the new available brands.

Coming on the market are all types of vodkas, made with increasingly interesting flavors that broaden the spectrum of cocktail components. Whisky, grappa, fruit brandies, rum - American distillers are producing a wealth of interesting spirits that add delightfully to bar menus. Take a look at the cocktail list on your next visit to one of these restaurants and keep your eye out for any new selections. Or ask the bartender about any intriguing new artisan spirits she might shake up for you. There can be as much adventure to be found in the bar as there is in the restaurant these days.

Purple Café & Wine Bar

Purple Café & Wine Bar is a multifaceted food and wine concept that merges casual sophistication with an upbeat metropolitan style. The restaurants feature a global wine selection, coupled with a menu that blends classic American styles, seasonal Northwest ingredients and Mediterranean themes. The atmosphere is often described as an urban retreat with rustic elements.

Warm Bucheron Goat Cheese with Dried Cranberries

Kitchen Note: Bucheron is an aged goat cheese from the Loire Valley in France that comes in the shape of a log. Look for it in specialty cheese shops and well-stocked grocery stores. If you're unable to find lemon thyme, you can use regular thyme with the addition of a pinch of finely grated lemon zest. You can use dried cherries or dried figs in place of the dried cranberries if you like.

Serves 6

10 to 12 ounces Bucheron goat cheese, cut into
    1/2 inch rounds
1/4 cup fireweed honey
3 tablespoons chopped dried cranberries
1 teaspoon lemon thyme leaves
Artisanal crackers, for serving

Preheat the oven to 400°F.

Lay the cheese rounds in a baking dish and bake until the cheese is bubbling and just beginning to brown, 6 to 8 minutes. Take the cheese from the oven and drizzle the honey over. Sprinkle some of the cranberries and lemon thyme over each round of cheese.

Transfer the cheese rounds to individual plates and serve warm, with crackers alongside.

serve your community while being served at Purple Café & Wine Bar!
visit www.celebratedchefs.com
www.thepurplecafe.com

Chef Robert Kirby and Culinary Director Harry Mills

Executive Chef Robert Kirby joined Purple Café & Wine Bar in 2001 as sous chef in Woodinville. He now oversees the kitchens and staff of all four Purple locations. Culinary Director Harry Mills is a graduate of the Art Institute of Seattle's School of Culinary Arts. He taught there for seven years and worked in many notable kitchens prior to joining Purple Café & Wine Bar.

Barking Frog

It's difficult to say what is most appealing about Barking Frog – the food, the wine, the atmosphere. All three have earned this casual bistro, which features wine country-inspired fresh Northwest cuisine, rave reviews. Delectable dishes entice guests to linger in the light-filled dining room or to gather around the fireplace. During the summer, lunch and dinner are served in the courtyard.

Grand Marnier Prawns

Kitchen Note: Dried orange zest is very easy to make at home. Peel away strips of zest (the orange part only, not the white pith underneath) from a navel orange and lay them on parchment paper on a baking sheet. Dry in a 200°F oven for 1 hour; turn off the oven and leave the baking sheet in the oven for an hour longer. Let cool, then grind the zest in a mortar and pestle or in a mini-processor. At Barking Frog these prawns are served with mixed greens that have been tossed with a lemongrass vinaigrette and mandarin oranges.

Serves 4

2 to 3 cups canola oil, for frying
20 prawns
Salt and freshly ground black pepper
1/2 cup corn starch, for dusting

Orange Sauce

1/4 cup Grand Marnier
1 cup freshly squeezed orange juice
1/2 cup mayonnaise
2 teaspoons finely ground, dried orange zest

For the sauce, put the Grand Marnier in a small saucepan and warm over medium heat, bringing it just to a boil to burn off the alcohol. Transfer the Grand Marnier to a small bowl and set aside. Add the orange juice to the saucepan and bring to a boil over medium-high heat. Reduce the heat to medium and boil until the juice is reduced to about 1/4 cup, 8 to 10 minutes. Take care that the reduction not burn around the edges of the pan; reduce the heat to medium-low if needed. Add the juice reduction to the Grand Marnier and set aside to cool completely. Stir in the mayonnaise and orange zest. Refrigerate until needed.

Pour enough canola oil into a medium, heavy saucepan to come about 2 inches up the sides (it should fill the pan no more than halfway). Heat the oil over medium heat to 350°F. While the oil is heating, season the prawns lightly with salt and pepper, then toss them in the cornstarch to evenly coat, patting to remove excess.

When the oil is heated, add about 1/4 of the prawns and fry until browned and crisp, about 2 minutes. Carefully lift them from the oil with a slotted spoon and set aside on paper towels to drain. Fry the remaining shrimp in batches, allowing the oil to reheat between batches as needed.

Put the shrimp in a medium bowl and toss them with the orange mayonnaise. Arrange the prawns on individual plates and serve.

serve your community while being
served at Barking Frog!
visit www.celebratedchefs.com
www.willowslodge.com

Chef Bobby Moore

Executive Chef Bobby Moore has been working in restaurants since the age of 15. Unparalleled attention to detail and a degree from Seattle Central Community College's culinary program brought him through the ranks from dishwasher to server and finally to the chef line at Fuller's restaurant in Seattle. Chef Moore began working at Barking Frog in 2001 and was named Executive Chef in April of 2005.

Andaluca

Dim lighting, dark mahogany, and lavish fabrics set the stage for an amazing meal at Andaluca, located in downtown Seattle's Mayflower Park Hotel. Spanish style tapas and pintxos lead a Mediterranean-inspired menu with a certain Northwest influence. Spices such as cumin, saffron, paprika and cinnamon produce a palate of unique and savory menu items, placing Andaluca on *Zagat's* list for one of *Seattle's Top Mediterranean Restaurants*.

Stuffed Dates

Kitchen Note: Chorizo is a highly seasoned pork sausage that tends to be spicy. It comes in two forms: raw (either in casings or bulk form) or cooked in casings (often smoked as well). In this case you want to use the raw, bulk form of chorizo.
Serves 6

2 tablespoons olive oil
3/4 cup finely chopped onion
2 teaspoons chopped garlic
6 ounces chorizo
1/4 teaspoon salt
1/8 teaspoon freshly ground black pepper
3 ounces chèvre or other fresh goat cheese,
    crumbled
30 pitted dates
2 tablespoons unsalted butter

Blood Orange Vinaigrette

1/2 cup olive oil
1/3 cup blood orange purée or orange juice
    concentrate
1 tablespoon honey
1/4 teaspoon salt

Salad

1 small head radicchio, leaves separated, rinsed,
    dried, and finely shredded
1 small head frisée, rinsed, tough outer leaves
    trimmed, and tender leaves separated
1 small carrot, julienned

Preheat the oven to 350°F.

Heat the olive oil in a large skillet over medium-low heat. Add the onion and garlic and cook, stirring occasionally, until tender and translucent, about 5 minutes. Add the chorizo, salt, and pepper and cook until the chorizo is fully cooked, 5 to 7 minutes, breaking the meat into small pieces as it cooks. Set aside in a fine-mesh strainer or on a paper towel to cool and drain. When cool, combine the chorizo mixture and chèvre in a medium bowl and stir until evenly blended. Use a small spoon to stuff each date with about 1 1/2 teaspoons of the chorizo filling. Set aside on a plate.

For the vinaigrette, combine the olive oil, orange purée, honey, and salt in a small bowl. Whisk to evenly blend.

Combine the radicchio, frisée, and carrot in a large bowl. Pour all but 1/4 cup of the vinaigrette over and toss to evenly mix. Arrange the salad to one side of individual plates. Spoon the remaining dressing in a line alongside the salad.

Heat the butter in a large oven-proof skillet over medium heat. Add the dates, stuffed-side up, and transfer the skillet to the oven. Bake the dates until heated through, 5 to 7 minutes. Use tongs to transfer the dates to the plates, setting them on top of the drizzle of vinaigrette. Serve right away.

Chef Wayne Johnson

Wayne Johnson has been Executive Chef of The Mayflower Park Hotel, Andaluca and Oliver's Lounge since 1999. After cooking his way through high school and college, Johnson started pursuing his culinary calling in 1981, working in Colorado and various San Francisco Bay Area hotels. Chef Johnson draws on special training in the foods of Spain from the Culinary Institute of America at Greystone, and is influenced by his mother's holiday feasts.

Ponti Seafood Grill

Nestled next to the historic Fremont Bridge with views of passing boats on the ship canal, Ponti celebrates the Northwest life. Elegantly appointed dining rooms offer unbeatable outdoor patio and water views. Northwest gifts of amazing seafood, meats, and incredible produce are created daily. Honors include *Gourmet's Top Table Award* and *Wine Spectator's Award of Excellence*.

Dungeness Crab Spring Rolls

Kitchen Note: It's important to use the right kind of wrapper here. You don't want an egg roll wrapper, which is thicker and smaller. Nor the rice paper wrapper used for fresh spring rolls, brittle when dry and softened in water before using. Here you will need wheat flour based spring roll wrappers that are 8 inches square, more delicate than egg roll wrappers. If you're unable to find this type of wrapper, you can use lumpia wrappers instead.

Makes 12 to 16 spring rolls

8 ounces fresh Dungeness crab meat, mixed claw
   and body
1/3 cup mayonnaise
3/4 teaspoon sambal oelek or other hot chile sauce
3 to 4 ounces thin rice stick noodles
1 cup finely julienned carrot
1 cup finely julienned green onions
1 cup finely shredded fresh basil
12 to 16 spring roll wrappers (see Kitchen Note)
1 egg white
2 to 3 cups canola or peanut oil, for frying
6 to 8 leaves romaine lettuce, tough stem removed
   and halved lengthwise
Sweet chili sauce, for dipping

Pick over the crab meat to remove any bits of shell or cartilage, then gently squeeze the meat to remove excess liquid. Stir together the crab, mayonnaise, and sambal oelek in a small bowl. Refrigerate until needed.

Soak the rice sticks in hot tap water until tender, about 10 minutes. Drain well and rinse with cold water. Drain again and cut noodles into 3- to 4-inch lengths. Refrigerate until needed.

Lay a spring roll wrapper on the counter with a corner toward you. Place roughly 1 tablespoon of the julienne carrot on the lower third of the wrapper, shaping it into a 3- x 1/2-inch pile. On the carrot, place about 1 tablespoon of the green onion, 1 tablespoon of the basil, and 1 tablespoon of the rice noodles. Top the noodles with 1 generous tablespoon of the crab mixture.

Fold in the sides of the wrapper to cover the filling, then fold up the bottom portion, nudging the filling into a compact bundle as you roll it upwards nearly to the top of the wrapper. Lightly brush the end corner with egg white to seal, and close the roll. Repeat with the remaining wrappers and filling ingredients.

Pour enough canola oil into a large, heavy saucepan to come about 2 inches up the sides (it should fill the pan no more than halfway). Heat the oil over medium heat to 360°F. Gently add 4 of the spring rolls and fry until nicely browned, 2 to 3 minutes. Gently turn the rolls a few times as they cook, so that they cook evenly. Lift the rolls out carefully with tongs or a basket strainer. Transfer to paper towels to drain while frying the

continued on page 34

serve your community while being served at Ponti seafood Grill!
visit www.celebratedchefs.com
www.pontiseafoodgrill.com

Chef Alvin Binuya

When Ponti Seafood Grill opened in 1990, Executive Chef Alvin Binuya commanded the kitchen, creating cutting-edge dishes that incorporated flavors without boundaries, now called fusion cuisine. As it enters its 20th year, Chef Alvin remains committed to providing Ponti's guests with the best ingredients from local producers, farmers and fishermen. Binuya showcases his talent with an ever-changing and seasonally focused menu.

continued from page 33

remaining rolls, allowing the oil to reheat between batches as needed.

Use a serrated knife to cut each roll in half at a slight angle. Wrap each portion in a piece of lettuce, securing the roll with a small bamboo pick. Arrange the rolls on individual plates, with a small dish of sweet chili sauce alongside for dipping.

Food & Wine Pairing

The interesting thing about wine pairing principles is that - while there are many resources that offer pointers, and wine experts are quick to offer ideal recommendations for your poached halibut with herb butter sauce or grilled duck breast with currants, the curious consumer is often told that ultimately, one can drink whatever they like with whatever they like. These rules for wine and food pairing were made, if not for breaking, at least for making personal amendments.

It is, after all, important to consider personal tastes and how widely divergent our preferences are for different flavors and combinations. As much as the "red wine with meat and white wine with fish" guideline seems well-founded, a lighter red, such as Grenache, can be an ideal partner for a fish dish. And rich, full-flavored white wine, the likes of an oaky Chardonnay or even a good dry oloroso sherry, can accompany a grilled steak.

That being said, there are sound principles to consider when selecting wine to go with your meal. You can choose one of two paths: complement or contrast. In a complementary context, the partner for a piece of pan-fried fish with a creamy or buttery sauce might be a rich, slightly aged Chardonnay. To contrast, the selection would lean toward a lighter, more acidic Sauvignon Blanc.

The more often-traveled path tends to be contrasting flavors in the glass with those on the plate. When the food and wine elements both lean toward the acidic or toward the rich, it can be a bit dulling to the palate - less dynamic than contrasting flavors would provide.

When you're making this choice while dining out, it's a great time to take advantage of the expertise of the restaurant team. Some restaurants have a staff person, the sommelier or wine director, dedicated to overseeing their wine selections and assisting customers with the task of choosing wines to accompany their meal. But many restaurants, too, make a point of educating their service staff, not only about the wine selections on their list, but also arming them with tools to help customers make a reliable selection for their meal.

Make some notes, mental or otherwise, about wine pairings that you particularly enjoy, and over time, you will have developed your own crib sheet for pairing selections that suit your own palate. Each new outing means more delicious research awaits, a lifelong pursuit.

Assaggio

From the moment you enter, the atmosphere is welcoming — the walls are painted with Michelangelo-inspired art, and the place buzzes with convivial chatter. You'll find Chef Mauro moving from table to table to ensure each diner's comfort and satisfaction. Assaggio presents a carefully composed menu of bold, robust central and northern Italian cuisine, which has consistently received accolades since first opening its doors.

Funghi Saltati
(Sautéed Wild Mushrooms)

Kitchen Note: When wild mushrooms aren't available, you can use crimini or other button mushrooms instead.

Serves 4 to 6

2 tablespoons olive oil
4 cloves garlic, minced
1 pound wild mushrooms, brushed clean and sliced
3 tablespoons slivered fresh basil leaves
1 teaspoon minced fresh rosemary
1/2 cup dry red wine
1/4 cup balsamic vinegar
2 tablespoons minced flat-leaf parsley
Sliced rustic bread, for serving

Heat the olive oil in a medium skillet over medium heat. Add the garlic and cook, stirring, until golden brown, about 1 minute. Add the mushrooms and cook until lightly browned, about 5 minutes, stirring occasionally.

Stir in the basil and rosemary, then reduce the heat to medium-low and cook until the wild mushrooms are tender, about 5 minutes. Add the wine and vinegar and simmer until the liquid is reduced by about half, 5 to 7 minutes.

Spoon the mushrooms into individual small bowls or ramekins and sprinkle the parsley over. Set the dishes on serving plates, with sliced bread alongside.

serve your community while being served at Assaggio!
visit www.celebratedchefs.com
www.assaggioseattle.com

Chef Mauro Golmarvi

Executive Chef and Owner Mauro Golmarvi grew up in Ancona, Italy, in the heart of the Marche region, renowned for its beauty and excellent cuisine. A self-taught chef with over 25 years of experience, Golmarvi worked in the Bay Area, then settled in Seattle in 1989, and started Assaggio Ristorante in 1993. Chef Golmarvi believes that the heart of good cooking is in "simplicity, honesty, and the freshest ingredients you can find. Food is an art, and we are the artists".

Wabi Sabi

Nestled in the Columbia City historical district, Wabi Sabi offers an intimate and contemporary dining experience. The menu focuses on fresh fish, traditional Japanese dishes and imported sake and beer. We use an innovative approach to the artistry of Japanese sushi and Pan Pacific Rim cuisine. Named after the Japanese art of celebrating simple and natural elegance, Wabi Sabi is a delightful dining experience and we look forward serving you.

Shoyu Ahi Poke Salad

Kitchen Note: Poke is a Hawaiian tradition of creative seafood salads, often raw, using a range of different types of seafoods and accent ingredients. This classic version is made using tuna and Japanese soy sauce, shoyu. Feel free to reduce the amount of sugar used in the dressing if you wish.

Serves 4

1/2 cup shoyu or other soy sauce
1 green onion, trimmed and thinly sliced
3 cloves garlic, finely chopped
2 tablespoons sugar
2 teaspoons sesame oil
1 teaspoon sambal oelek or other hot chile sauce
1 pound fresh sashimi-grade tuna, cut into 3/4 inch
  cubes
1/2 cup finely diced English cucumber
1/4 cup thinly sliced red onion

Combine the shoyu, green onion, garlic, sugar, sesame oil, and sambal oelek in a medium bowl and whisk until the sugar is dissolved. Add the tuna, cucumber, and red onion and stir to evenly mix. Cover and refrigerate for 30 minutes. Spoon the poke salad onto individual plates and serve.

serve your community while being
served at Wabi Sabi!

visit www.celebratedchefs.com
www.wabisabicolumbiacity.com

Chef John Gaffud

Raised in the Phillipines, Executive Chef John Gaffud, gained an appreciation for food and cooking at a very young age. After spending time cooking in Los Angeles, Chef Gaffud arrived in Seattle, and has been creating sushi for local diners since 2002. Chef Gaffud appreciates the aesthetic of sushi-making, the art of food presentation and the clean taste of high-quality ingredients. It is at Wabi Sabi that Chef Gaffud shares his passion with you.

Voilà!

Voilà! reigns as Seattle's quintessential Parisian-style bistro experience, combining honest, comfortable French cooking in an inviting and festive atmosphere. Situated in Madison Valley, guests can enjoy classic French fare as Coq au Vin, Boeuf Bourguignon, and Crème Brûlée. Whether you are with someone special or having a casual dinner with friends, Voila! is an ideal destination for any occasion.

Moules au Bleu d'Auvergne

Serves 2

2 pounds live Penn Cove or Mediterranean mussels,
    scrubbed and debearded
1/4 cup dry white wine
1/4 cup heavy cream
1 ounce Bleu d'Auvergne or other French blue
    cheese, crumbled
2 tablespoons finely chopped white onion
Salt and freshly ground black pepper
Chopped flat-leaf parsley, for serving

Put the mussels in a large sauté pan or medium pot. Add the wine, cream, cheese, and onion with a good pinch each of salt and pepper. Cover the pan and bring to a boil over medium-high heat. Cook, shaking the pan gently once or twice, until the mussels have opened, about 5 minutes.

Use a slotted spoon to transfer the mussels to shallow bowls. Boil the cooking liquids to thicken slightly, 1 to 2 minutes. Spoon the sauce over the mussels, sprinkle with the parsley, and serve.

serve your community while being served at Voilà!

visit www.celebratedchefs.com
www.voilabistro.com

Chef Laurent Gabrel

Chef and Owner Laurent Gabrel was born and raised in Paris, and attended the Cooking School of Versailles. He moved to the U.S. in 1987 and worked in top kitchens across the country before landing in Seattle. Locally, Gabrel has opened many restaurants, Chloé Bistrot in Laurelhurst being his newest. "Voilà!" he says, "is the only French word you don't have to speak French to remember".

Barrio

Barrio, which means community, is an approachable and inviting representation of modern Mexico. Here, the menu takes a Northwest approach to Mexican-inspired cuisine, punctuated by cocktails that are creative, classic, and Latin-focused. The scene is lively and the restaurant thrives on the street energy provided by the local neighborhoods they are pleased to call their "barrio."

Three Salsas: Fresh Tomato, Roasted Habanero and Roasted Tomatillo-Serrano

Kitchen Note: Tomatillos contain a lot of natural pectin, which makes the salsa gel in the fridge. This is normal, just stir it well to "break" the gel. Resist the urge to further thin it with water, which will dilute the flavor of the salsa. Leaving the seeds in the serrano chiles for the roasted tomatillo salsa will provide a maximum of heat level; if you prefer the salsa to be a bit milder, remove the seeds before using the chiles. Habanero chiles are among the hottest out there, you should wear gloves while working with the chiles.

Serves 6 to 8

Roasted Tomatillo-Serrano Salsa

2 to 3 serrano chiles, cored
4 cloves garlic
2 1/2 pounds tomatillos, husks removed
Agave nectar, as needed
Salt

Fresh Tomato Salsa

2 pints grape tomatoes
   (or small heirloom tomatoes when in season)
1 jalapeño chile, cored, seeded, and finely diced
1 Fresno chile, cored, seeded, and finely diced
Juice of 3 key limes or 2 regular limes
1/3 cup finely diced red onion
3 tablespoons chopped fresh cilantro
1 tablespoon agave nectar
Salt

Roasted Habanero Salsa

3 cloves garlic (in their skins)
2 to 4 habanero chiles
1 can (28 ounces) fire roasted tomatoes
2 tablespoons key lime juice or regular lime juice
1 tablespoon agave nectar

Preheat the oven to 475°F.

To make the Roasted Tomatillo-Serrano Salsa:
Put the garlic cloves and chiles in a baking dish and top them with the tomatillos. Roast in the oven until the skins are blistered and slightly blackened and the tomatillos are tender, 8 to 12 minutes. Let cool slightly, then purée the tomatillos, chiles, and garlic in a food processor until nearly smooth, adding a bit of water if needed. Transfer to a serving bowl and season to taste with agave nectar and salt.

To make the Fresh Tomato Salsa:
Put the tomatoes in a food processor and pulse just to coarsely chop them to a chunky texture (do not fully purée the tomatoes). Transfer the tomatoes to a medium

continued on page 44

serve your community while being served at Barrio!
visit www.celebratedchefs.com
www.barriorestaurant.com

Chef Kristin Mills

Executive Chef Kristin Mills brings a wide range of culinary experience to Barrio. As a graduate of the Art Institute of Seattle's School of Culinary Arts, she honed her skills at Cutter's Bayhouse, The Pink Door, Fira, and most recently, at Café Campagne. Chef Mills has a knack for ethnic cooking, making her the perfect fit for Barrio's Northwest-inspired Mexican cuisine.

continued from page 43

bowl and stir in the jalapeño chile, Fresno chile, lime juice, onion, cilantro, and agave nectar. Season to taste with salt. Spoon the salsa into a sieve or colander set in a bowl and drain for at least 1 hour. (You can save the drained liquid for another use, such as in a soup or chili, or part of a bloody mary.) Just before serving, check the salsa for seasoning, adding more salt, lime juice, or agave nectar to taste.

To make the Roasted Habanero Salsa:
Put the garlic cloves in a small, heavy skillet and toast over medium-high heat until their skins are nearly black, 3 to 5 minutes. Set aside to cool, then peel the garlic.

Roast the habanero chiles over a gas flame or under the broiler until the skin is blistered and partly blackened. Let cool, then remove the stems and peel away the charred skin; discard the seeds, too, to moderate the heat if you like.

Combine the tomatoes, chiles, garlic, lime juice, and agave nectar in a food processor and pulse until finely chopped and well blended. The salsa can have a bit of a chunky texture. Transfer the salsa to a serving bowl. Taste for seasoning, adding salt and more agave nectar to taste.

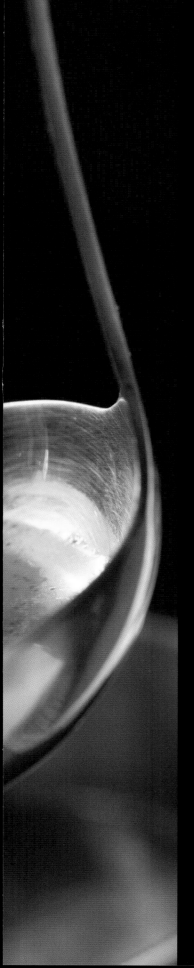

Food and Service

There's something extraordinary about the hospitality industry. While people from all walks of life do what they can to support the communities where they live, those in the restaurant world tend to do so at an amplified level.

It comes down to the fact that food and service have long been such an important partnership. Food is, of course, integral to the human experience. And it is also a restaurant's stock-in-trade. It is only natural, then, that food becomes a means by which chefs and restaurateurs interact with the community well beyond their businesses' walls. Yes, they serve patrons with enticing food in an inviting setting. But they also serve those who may never patronize their restaurants. It's part of the greater scope of hospitality, generously supporting neighbors with their time and talents. Not only have these chefs and restaurateurs committed to supporting regional charities by way of the Celebrated Chefs program, donating up to 5% of every dining experience back to your chosen cause, they also contribute to the community in ways that you may never realize. They're tapped for countless auctions and other fundraisers each year - to cook, to donate food, to provide auction items. Chefs also host fundraisers in their own restaurants, forgoing a night's dinner receipts to, instead, turn income over to a special charity.

Many chefs participate in national organizations that work to end hunger, such as Share Our Strength. Others give their time to serve as guest chefs for special classes or events that raise funds for worthy causes. And chefs rally like nobody's business when disaster calls. Feeding survivors and volunteers in the wakes of Hurricane Katrina and 9-11 are phenomenal examples of the boundless generosity that chefs share. All this on top of keeping things simmering along in their own restaurants.

It's one reason that Celebrated Chefs is so happy to be working in partnership with these restaurant chefs. We salute them and all that they already do to support those in need, both near and far. The more you dine in their establishments, the greater the funds raised to support non-profit groups. Let's support those chefs who give so generously.

CREATIVE AND TASTY COMBINATIONS CONTINUE THE THEME

This chapter includes a delicious variety of recipes you can serve guests at the start of a meal, or as part of the main course. In fact some of these tempting recipes, served in larger portions, could just as well be the centerpiece of the meal, with crusty – perhaps even garlicky – bread served alongside.

Each season - fall, winter, spring and summer – there are soups and salads that seem to represent the weather, be it garden-fresh light or robust and hearty. Celebrated Chefs make a point of preparing these recipes at the peak of their season to create standout results. You can accomplish the same results by choosing recipes that are representative of the season like apples and butternut squash in the fall, mushrooms and peas in the spring or berries and corn in the summer. Visit your local farmers markets to source the freshest ingredients and you will be rewarded with results that mimic the chefs.

www.celebratedchefs.com

SOUPS AND SALADS

POPPY

Poppy's warm, modern dining room looks out to the vibrant streetscape of North Capitol Hill. Come for a "thali" - a platter served to each guest holding a variety of small dishes - like a tasting menu served all at once. The thali changes daily, highlighting Chef Jerry's acclaimed style of innovative Northwest cooking. Or visit Poppy to enjoy carefully mixed cocktails and lighter dining in our lively bar/lounge.

Poppy Chickpea Salad

Kitchen Note: This boldly flavored salad will be a terrific accompaniment to a backyard barbecue. Toasting the spices is an important step as it transforms their flavor remarkably, but be careful not to let them get too dark. If using canned chickpeas, you'll need about 1 1/2 cans; drain and rinse the chickpeas well before using. Starting from dried chickpeas will give you a clearer flavor; 3/4 dried chickpeas simmered in 4 cups of water for about 1 1/2 hours will provide you about the 2 cups needed here.

Serves: 4 to 6

2 cups cooked chickpeas
2 tablespoons peanut oil or vegetable oil
1 teaspoon brown mustard seeds
1/2 teaspoon cumin seeds
1/4 teaspoon ajwain seeds, fennel seeds, or
    celery seeds
1/8 to 1/4 teaspoon dried red pepper flakes
1/2 cup chopped green onions
1/4 cup chopped fresh cilantro
1 tablespoon freshly squeezed lemon juice
3/4 teaspoon sea salt, such as Fleur de Sel or
    Malden salt
1/2 cup whole milk plain yogurt

Put the chickpeas in a medium bowl.

Heat the oil in a small skillet over medium-high heat. When the oil is hot, add the mustard seeds and quickly cover the pan partially with a lid to shield the sputtering seeds, then turn the heat to low. When the sputtering subsides, after about 30 seconds, remove the lid and add the cumin, ajwain, and pepper flakes and cook, stirring, until the spices are a deeper brown and fragrant, 10 to 15 seconds.

Immediately pour the oil and spices over the chickpeas. Add the green onion, cilantro, lemon juice, and salt and toss with a rubber spatula to evenly mix. Stir in the yogurt. Serve right away, or refrigerate for up to 3 or 4 hours before serving. Allow to come to room temperature before serving.

serve your community while being
served at Poppy!
visit www.celebratedchefs.com
www.poppyseattle.com

Chef Jerry Traunfeld

Prior to opening Poppy, Chef and Owner Jerry Traunfeld was Executive Chef of the highly acclaimed Herbfarm Restaurant. Garnering national attention for his seasonal menus and expertise in herbs, he won the *James Beard Award* for *Best Chef, Northwest* in 2000. In addition to countless articles and television appearances, Jerry was most recently on *Top Chef Masters. He* is also the author of two award-winning cookbooks, *The Herbfarm Cookbook* and *The Herbal Kitchen.*

Crow

Crow Restaurant & Bar has been a neighborhood "hot spot" for the past five years. Located in the Theatre District of Lower Queen Anne, Crow offers a seasonal, rotating menu in an urban and energetic dining environment. Housed in a 100 year-old warehouse, Crow's exterior is a stunning mixture of rusted metal and brick. The open kitchen and Chef's Counter are favorite seats for the neighborhood regulars.

Vanilla-Scented Carrot Bisque

Serves 6 to 8

2 cups half-and-half
2 to 3 vanilla beans, split lengthwise
2 tablespoons unsalted butter
2 pounds carrots, chopped
1 medium leek, split, cleaned, and chopped
4 cups chicken stock or broth, more if needed
1/4 cup crème fraîche or sour cream, plus more
   for serving
Chopped chives, for serving
Salt

Bring the half-and-half to a low simmer in a medium saucepan. Run the tip of a small knife down the length of each vanilla bean half to remove the tiny seeds. Add the seeds and the beans to the half-and-half and take the pan from the heat. Let steep until needed.

Melt the butter in a medium soup pot over medium heat. Add carrots and leek and cook until the vegetables are tender and aromatic, 5 to 7 minutes. Add the chicken stock and strain the half-and-half into the pot as well. Press on the vanilla beans with a rubber spatula to extract as much flavor from them as you can; discard the beans.

Bring the stock to a low boil over medium heat, then reduce the heat to low. Simmer until the carrots are very soft, 15 to 17 minutes. Let cool slightly then, working in 3 to 4 batches, purée the bisque in a blender until smooth, adding the crème fraîche divided among the batches.

Return the bisque to the pot and gently reheat. Season to taste with salt. Ladle the bisque into warmed soup bowl and garnish with a swirl of crème fraîche and a sprinkling of chives.

serve your community while being
served at Crow!

visit www.celebratedchefs.com
www.eatatcrow.com

Chef Craig Serbousek

Formally trained in Chicago, Chef and Owner Craig Serbousek has been in the Seattle restaurant scene for 15 years. After working in some of Seattle's finest restaurants, he opened his first neighborhood restaurant called Stumbling Goat Bistro. In 2004, he opened Crow Restaurant and Bar. Since then, he has introduced a sister restaurant, Betty. Craig's philosophy is simply prepared, comforting dishes, utilizing the natural flavors of seasonal ingredients.

Palisade

You may first notice the rustic timbers and salt water ponds, but you'll leave remembering the exquisite dining experience that Palisade inspires. Join us for an expertly prepared meal that seamlessly blends flavors from across the Pacific, and you'll understand why Palisade is Seattle's Pacific icon. The combination of breathtaking views and unparalleled waterfront dining, makes Palisade a signature landmark for all occasions.

Bibb Lettuce Salad with Blue Cheese and Butter Poached Smoked Prawns

Kitchen Kitchen Note: The delicious prawns served on this signature salad are both butter-poached and smoked. The latter adds a touch of lovely smoky flavor, but that step can be skipped and you'll still have wonderful results. This is a good time to use a top-quality blue cheese, such as Rogue River Oregon Blue.

Serves 2

1 head bibb lettuce, rinsed, dried, and
   leaves separated
2 tablespoons chopped toasted hazelnuts
1/4 cup crumbled blue cheese
5 cherry or grape tomatoes, halved
1/4 cup julienned ripe pear
4 Butter Poached Smoked Prawns

Blue Cheese Dressing

2 tablespoons red wine vinegar
1/2 teaspoon Worcestershire sauce
1/2 teaspoon minced garlic
1/4 teaspoon dry mustard
1/4 teaspoon freshly ground black pepper
1/4 teaspoon onion salt
1 cup mayonnaise
1/3 cup sour cream
3 tablespoons buttermilk
1/3 cup crumbled blue cheese

Butter Poached Smoked Prawns

1 tablespoon water
1 pound salted butter, cut into pieces and chilled
4 large prawns, peeled and deveined
1 cup wood smoking chips
   (such apple, guava, or cherry)

For the dressing, combine the red wine vinegar, Worcestershire sauce, garlic, mustard, black pepper, and onion salt until evenly blended and the salt has dissolved. Add the mayonnaise, sour cream, and buttermilk and whisk until fully blended and creamy. Fold in the blue cheese crumbles with a rubber spatula so the dressing stays chunky.

For the prawns, put the water in a shallow saucepan and bring just to a boil over medium heat. Reduce the heat to low and add a few pieces of the butter and whisk until melted. Continue adding a few more pieces of butter at a time and whisking until melted before adding the next. You'll have an emulsified butter sauce when done. Transfer the butter to the top of a double boiler. Add the prawns and cook gently over simmering, not boiling,

continued on page 54

serve your community while being
served at Palisade!

visit www.celebratedchefs.com
www.palisaderestaurant.com

Chef Chris Bryant

A Washington native who enjoys spending time with his young son and his beautiful wife, Executive Chef Chris Bryant is a graduate of Washington State University with a bachelor's degree in Hotel & Restaurant Administration. His approach to cooking is focused on fresh ingredients and flawless execution.

continued from page 53

water until they are evenly opaque, 8 to 12 minutes. Lift out the prawns and drain on paper towel, then refrigerate until ready to smoke.

Soak the wood chips in water for 1 hour.

Light a smoker or preheat an outdoor grill for indirect heat, tossing the wood chips on the coals. Set the shrimp on the grate, cover the smoker or grill (closing all vents), and smoke for 6 to 8 minutes. The heat level should be relatively low, as the shrimp are already cooked and the goal is to add smoky flavor rather than cook them more.

Place the whole bibb lettuce leaves, overlapping slightly, in the center of large individual plates. Drizzle a few tablespoons of the dressing over each salad (extra dressing will keep for one week in the refrigerator). Sprinkle the hazelnuts, tomato, and blue cheese crumbles over and around the lettuce. Add the pear in a mound the center of the lettuce and set the prawns on top of the pear. Serve right away.

Olive Oil and Company

Olive oil has become such a common kitchen ingredient that some cooks simply use it for everything from vinaigrette to stir-frying. And the nice thing about olive oil is that it is just that versatile, even showing up in desserts such as extra-moist olive oil cakes.

There are two camps when it comes to cooking with extra virgin olive oil. "Extra virgin" is the oil that is the result of a cold first-pressing of the olives, resulting in the most flavorful, elegant oils of lowest acidity. Ranging in color from dark straw to deep green, these oils have robust, pronounced flavors. Typically for cooking, you opt for a somewhat neutral oil that doesn't overpower food flavors. But when that added flavor is something as delicious as extra virgin olive oil, it can be a welcome addition.

So go ahead and use extra virgin to sauté vegetables or shrimp. The lower the acidity, the higher the smoke point (the temperature at which the oil begins to give off smoke, generally to be avoided). The drawback is that extra virgin oil also tends to be the most expensive of the olive oils. It's why many cooks prefer to keep their premium extra virgin bottles to use as "finishing oils," which means they get drizzled over a dish just before serving, or are saved for vinaigrette dressings and other showcase uses.

A "virgin" olive oil is generally from a first pressing as well, but later in the season when riper olives produce oils of higher acidity. These are still solid candidates for cooking oils, with milder flavors that can be a bit more versatile, such as for deep-frying.

Further processing or refining of lower quality or higher acidity products results in oils that are blended with virgin or extra virgin oil, and labeled simply as "olive oil" or "pure olive oil." These are good for everyday cooking, but less optimal as finishing oils.

Some chefs like to use a combination oil for high-heat cooking. Making their own blend of olive oil with a more neutral vegetable oil (often in 50/50 proportions) allows them to gain the benefit of flavor from the olive oil with the higher smoke point of a vegetable oil. This is particularly valuable when cooking over the extreme heat that restaurant stoves can attain.

La Spiga

Pietro Borghesi and Sabrina Tinsley have been acclaimed for their hospitality and commitment to serving the simple, delicious cuisine of Emilia-Romagna. Cool enough for a date and warm enough to bring the family, the artfully designed 6,000 square foot Capitol Hill landmark features a massive bar, backed by an impressive wine collection. The menu reflects the traditions of Emilia-Romagna integrated with the bounty of the Northwest.

Vellutata di Patate
(Potato and Saffron Soup)

Serves 6 to 8

2 tablespoons unsalted butter
2 leeks, white and pale green parts only, split,
    cleaned, and sliced
4 large yellow potatoes, about 2 pounds, peeled
    and cut into wedges
1 cup dry white wine
1 1/2 quarts veal or beef stock or broth
1 bay leaf, preferably fresh
Salt
2 pinches saffron threads (optional)
1 cup whipping cream
1 tablespoon curry powder
2 tablespoons minced flat-leaf parsley, plus more
    for serving

Melt the butter in a large saucepan over medium heat.
Add the leeks and cook, stirring often, until tender,
about 5 minutes. Add the potatoes and cook for 5
minutes longer, stirring occasionally. Add the wine and
bring to a boil. Simmer until the liquid is reduced by
half, 3 to 5 minutes.

Add all but 1/2 cup of the veal stock to the pan (or add
all the veal stock if not using the saffron). Add the bay
leaf and a good pinch of salt and bring the stock to a
boil. Reduce the heat to medium and simmer until the
potatoes are quite tender when pierced with the tip of a
knife, 12 to 15 minutes.

While the potatoes are simmering, warm the reserved
stock in a small saucepan over medium heat. Take the
pan from the heat and add the saffron; set aside to
steep.

Remove the bay leaf from the soup, then purée it until
smooth, in a food processor or with an immersion
blender. Add the saffron-broth mixture, the cream, curry
powder, and parsley to the soup. Reheat the soup over
medium heat and taste for seasoning, adding more salt
if needed.

Ladle the soup into individual bowls, add a sprinkling of
minced parsley, and serve.

serve your community while being
served at La Spiga!
visit www.celebratedchefs.com
www.laspiga.com

Chef Sabrina Tinsley

Chef and Co-owner Sabrina Tinsley's passion for food was
cultivated early in life, while watching her mother cook from the
treasures of the family garden. Chef Tinsley spent five years in
Italy cooking alongside home cooks, studying the styles of Italian
chefs, and gaining an intimate knowledge of the traditional
cuisine of Emilia-Romagna, a foundation she follows adamantly.
Praised for her skill and creativity, Sabrina has been featured on
numerous television and radio programs and as a key speaker in
various food forums and fund-raising events.

Chez Shea

Perched above the bustling crowds of Pike Place Market with stunning views of Elliott Bay and the Olympic Mountains, sits Chez Shea. This intimate restaurant features Northwest ingredients served in the style of contemporary French cuisine. Detailed service, candlelit tables, and meticulously crafted meals, invite guests to indulge in both the romance and impressive cooking of Chef Knutsen's French-inspired Northwest menu.

Apple, Radicchio and Roasted Squash Salad

Serves 6

1 small butternut squash, about 1 1/2 pounds
5 tablespoons cider vinegar
2 tablespoon honey
Salt and freshly ground black pepper
1/3 cup canola oil
1 apple, cored, halved, and thinly sliced
1 head radicchio, leaves separated, rinsed, dried, and coarsely chopped
1/3 cup chopped hazelnuts (toasted and skinned)
5 ounces Fourme d'Ambert or other blue cheese, crumbled

Preheat the oven to 350°F.

Halve the squash lengthwise and scoop out the seeds. Peel the squash and cut it into 1/4-inch thick slices. For pieces wider than about 1/2 inch, halve them lengthwise into thinner strips. Put the squash in a medium bowl and toss well with 1 tablespoon of the vinegar, 1 tablespoon of the honey, and a pinch each of salt and pepper. Scatter the squash in a single layer in a baking dish and roast until tender but still holding its shape, 20 to 30 minutes. Set aside to cool.

For the vinaigrette dressing, combine the remaining 4 tablespoons of the cider vinegar, 1 tablespoon of the honey, and the oil in a small bowl. Whisk to blend and season to taste with salt and pepper.

Put the roasted squash in a large bowl and add the apple, radicchio, hazelnuts, and vinaigrette. Toss gently to evenly mix. Arrange the salads on individual plates, scatter the blue cheese over, and serve.

serve your community while being
served at Chez Shea!

visit www.celebratedchefs.com
www.chezshea.com

Chef Benjamin Knutsen

Benjamin Knutsen worked for and learned from French master chefs at top-rated restaurants in Portland and San Francisco before joining Chez Shea as Executive Chef. There, he honed his French cooking skills and precision in the kitchen. His signature dishes combine French technique with NorthWest flavor, which complement the tradition and ambience that has made Chez Shea one of Seattle's most romantic and treasured destinations.

shuckers

Boasting the beautifully carved oak paneling and unique tin ceiling of the haberdashery it once was in the 1930s, Shuckers is one of Seattle's oldest and most preeminent seafood restaurants. With a daily menu featuring a selection of fresh fish and seafood, Shuckers brims with 13 different kinds of oysters, and features local artisan microbrews.

Seafood Chowder

Note: The rich, complex flavors of this chowder echo, somewhat, the character of a gumbo from New Orleans. That bit of gumbo filé—ground sassafras—contributes quite a lot to that NOLA effect. Look for it in specialty spice shops and in the spice aisle of well-stocked grocery stores.

Serves 8

2 tablespoons vegetable oil
3/4 cup diced onion
1/2 cup diced red bell pepper
1/2 cup diced green bell pepper
1/2 cup diced celery
1 tablespoon minced garlic
1 tablespoon unsalted butter
1/2 teaspoon dried thyme
1/2 teaspoon dried oregano
1 bay leaf, preferably fresh
1/2 teaspoon paprika
1/2 teaspoon salt
1/4 teaspoon cayenne pepper
1/4 teaspoon ground white pepper
3 tablespoon gumbo file
2 cups diced tomatoes, fresh or drained canned
1 cup tomato purée
2 quarts fish stock (see page 83)
3/4 cup dry white wine
8 ounces red potatoes, diced
8 ounces halibut or other firm white fish, diced
8 ounces Dungeness crab meat
8 ounces bay shrimp

Heat the oil in a soup pot over medium-high heat. Add the onion, bell peppers, and celery and cook, stirring often, until tender, 5 to 7 minutes. Add the filé, garlic, butter, thyme, oregano, bay leaf, paprika, salt, cayenne, and white pepper, and cook, stirring, until the butter is melted. Add the diced tomatoes, tomato purée, and wine, then stir in 1 quart of the fish stock.

Bring the liquid to a boil over medium-high heat. Add the remaining fish stock and return to a boil. Simmer until the liquid is reduced by about one quarter, about 30 minutes. Reduce the heat to medium, add the potatoes and cook gently until the potatoes are tender, 10 to 12 minutes. Remove the bay leaf and discard.

Add the halibut, crab, and shrimp to the chowder and cook gently just until warmed through and the halibut is fully cooked, 2 to 3 minutes. Ladle the chowder into individual bowls and serve.

serve your community while being served at shuckers!
visit www.celebratedchefs.com
www.fairmont.com/seattle

Chef Gavin Stephenson

Gavin Stephenson has been Executive Chef of The Fairmont Olympic Hotel since 1999. Chef Stephenson has received numerous awards and accolades. The Georgian and Shuckers continue to receive critical acclaim and praise under his leadership. His relationships with local seafood and organic produce purveyors ensures patrons that Shuckers serves only the freshest ingredients.

Carmelita

Inspired by their love of life, art, food and family, proprietors Kathryn Neumann and Michael Hughes created Carmelita, named after Michael's mother. As Seattle's premier vegetarian restaurant, Carmelita supports independent farmers and foragers and uses organic ingredients whenever possible to create a plentiful, delightful feast. From summer's heirloom tomatoes to the golden squash of winter, everyone welcomes the changing seasons at Carmelita.

Watercress Salad, Roasted Apples, Bleu Cheese and Roasted Macadamia Nuts with Apple Cider Vinaigrette

Serves 6

3 Fuji apples, cored and quartered
3 to 4 tablespoons vegetable oil
1/2 cup roasted whole macadamia nuts
1/4 cup crumbled good blue cheese (such as English Stilton)
6 to 8 ounces watercress, trimmed, rinsed, and dried

Apple Cider Vinaigrette

1/2 cup apple cider
1/4 cup olive oil
2 shallots, minced
1 teaspoon fresh thyme leaves
2 tablespoons apple cider vinegar
Salt and freshly ground black pepper

Preheat the oven to 350°F.

Put the apples in a large bowl and toss with enough vegetable oil to lightly and evenly coat the apple. Season with salt and pepper, then arrange the apples in a roasting pan or on a rimmed baking sheet. Roast until aromatic and tender, 6 to 10 minutes. Set aside to cool.

For the vinaigrette, bring the apple cider to a boil in a small saucepan and boil until reduced by half, 3 to 5 minutes. Set aside to cool. Heat 1 tablespoon of the olive oil in a small skillet over medium heat. Add the shallots and thyme and cook, stirring occasionally, until tender and translucent, 2 to 3 minutes. Set aside to cool. Put the cooled shallot/thyme mixture in a blender with the reduced cider, remaining olive oil, cider vinegar, and a pinch each of salt and pepper. Blend until smooth and transfer to a small bowl. Taste for seasoning, adding more salt or pepper taste.

Put the watercress in a large bowl, drizzle the dressing over, and toss to evenly coat. Arrange the greens on individual plates, top with the roasted apple pieces, macadamia nuts, and blue cheese. Serve right away.

serve your community while being served at Carmelita!

visit www.celebratedchefs.com
www.carmelita.net

Chef Carlos Caula

Executive Chef Carlos Caula joined Carmelita in early 2009. A native of Cuba and a graduate of Le Cordon Bleu in London, he has worked in top restaurants in Colombia, South America, and the U.S. His passion for food and farm-to-table philosophy is evident in his attention to detail, combination of complex flavors, and artful presentations. Chef Carlos brings his energy and enthusiasm to create a collaborative environment with the Carmelita crew.

Le Gourmand

Since opening the doors in 1985, Chef Naftaly has personally attended to the details of every dish in the kitchen of Le Gourmand. Personalization, quality, and presentation are just as important as the organic, locally sourced ingredients. This unassuming French restaurant, tucked away in the Ballard neighborhood, combines an intimate dining experience with a thoughtful menu, providing one unforgettable evening after another.

Jerusalem Artichoke and Sorrel Soup

Kitchen Note: The puréed Jerusalem artichokes (also known as sunchokes) give this soup a creamy texture as it is, but for an added touch of richness you can add 1/4 cup of whipping cream to the soup at the end. Note that the cut artichokes begin to discolor quickly, plan to put them directly into a bowl of cold water to avoid discoloring while you're preparing them.

Serves 4

1 tablespoon unsalted butter
1 small onion, diced
1 leek, white portion only, split, rinsed, and diced
1 shallot, diced
3 cups chicken stock or broth
3/4 pound Jerusalem artichokes, scrubbed and cut into small pieces
1 ounce fresh sorrel , rinsed, dried, and cut into thin strips
Salt and freshly ground white pepper

Melt the butter in a large saucepan over medium-low heat. Add the onion, leek, and shallot and cook gently until they are translucent and tender, about 15 minutes. The onions should not brown, reduce the heat if needed.

Add the stock and Jerusalem artichokes to the pan, cover, and bring just to a boil over medium-high heat. Reduce the heat to medium-low and simmer until the Jerusalem artichokes are soft, 20 to 25 minutes. Set aside to cool slightly, then purée the soup in batches in a blender or in a food processor (the blender will give you the smoothest results).

Return the soup to the saucepan (you can press it through a sieve for an extra smooth texture), stir in the sorrel,and cook over medium-low heat until the sorrel is cooked and the soup is well heated, about 5 minutes. Season to taste with salt and pepper and serve.

serve your community while being served at Le Gourmand!

visit www.celebratedchefs.com
www.legourmandrestaurant.com

Chef Bruce Naftaly & Chef Sara Naftaly

In 1976, a passionate interest in French cooking led Chef Bruce Naftaly to a position as a dishwasher at the legendary Rossellini's Other Place, where he became head chef just one year later. Chef Naftaly opened Le Gourmand in 1985. He and wife, Chef Sara Naftaly, collaborate in passing on their love for French cuisine to every guest who visits. They agree that cooking is an art and that eating is a wonderful necessity.

photo courtesy of Bob Peterson

Ten Mercer

When guests head into Ten Mercer, they can expect flavorful and artfully presented foods, classic cocktails, and an award winning wine list, all served by a professional staff. Located near several of Seattle's top theaters as well as McCaw Hall, and the Key Arena, this Queen Anne neighborhood dinner house is the perfect stop before or after an event.

Wild Green Salad with Stilton Vinaigrette

Kitchen Note: At Ten Mercer, Chef Doug Wilson grills the pear slices before adding them to the salad. You may not want to fire up the grill at home just for that purpose; simply using fresh pear slices is a delicious alternative.

Serves 4

2 ounces thinly sliced pancetta
8 ounces seasonal greens, preferably local and
   organic, rinsed and dried
16 candied (see page 153) or toasted pecan halves
2 medium grapefruit, segmented (see page 153)
1 ripe but firm pear, cored and cut into eighths
Thinly slivered red bell pepper, for serving

Stilton Vinaigrette

3 tablespoons red wine vinegar
1 1/2 teaspoons Dijon mustard
1 1/2 teaspoons freshly squeezed lemon juice
1 teaspoon sugar
1/8 teaspoon black pepper
1/8 teaspoon minced garlic
1/2 cup extra virgin olive oil
2 ounces Stilton or other blue cheese, crumbled

For the vinaigrette, combine the vinegar, Dijon mustard, lemon juice, sugar, pepper, and garlic in a medium bowl and whisk until the sugar has dissolved. While whisking, add the olive oil in a slow stream. Add the Stilton and whisk to evenly blend. Set aside.

Heat a large nonstick skillet over medium heat. Add the pancetta slices and cook until browned and crisp, 3 to 5 minutes, turning the slices a few times. Transfer the pancetta to paper towels to cool. When cool, break the pancetta into small pieces.

Put the greens in a large bowl and pour the vinaigrette over. Toss to mix evenly and arrange the greens in the centers of individual plates. Set the pecan halves, grapefruit segments, and pear slices around the outer edge of the salad. Scatter the pancetta pieces over, top with a pinch of slivered bell pepper, and serve.

serve your community while being served at Ten Mercer!

visit www.celebratedchefs.com
www.tenmercer.com

Chef Doug Wilson

Doug Wilson has been the Executive Chef of Ten Mercer since 2004. Ten Mercer offers him a great opportunity to showcase his creativity through monthly wine dinners and special menus for charitable events. Chef Wilson lives in West Seattle with his wife Briony, and his two dogs.

Nell's

Nell's is an intimate, chef-owned restaurant located in the vibrant Green Lake neighborhood. Open for dinner seven nights a week, Nell's offers European-inspired New American cuisine featuring the finest Northwest seasonal ingredients. Diners at Nell's can choose from our current seasonal fare, or enjoy our sumptuous five-course tasting menu. Nell's menus are designed to pair beautifully with your wine selection from our hand-picked wine list.

White Corn Soup with Cumin Seed Oil and Mint

Kitchen Note: You'll get fuller, more distinctive cumin flavor in this recipe if you start with whole seeds, toast them lightly and grind them yourself. In a pinch, you can use pre-ground cumin if you wish.

Serves 8

2 tablespoons unsalted butter
1 cup chopped onion
4 1/2 cups chicken stock or broth, more if needed
6 cups freshly cut white corn kernels
   (from 6 to 8 ears)
Salt and freshly ground black pepper
1 teaspoon cumin seeds, toasted and ground
2 tablespoons extra virgin olive oil
1 tablespoon thinly slivered mint

Melt the butter in a medium soup pot over medium heat. Add the onion and cook until tender and translucent, about 5 minutes. Add the stock and bring just to a boil over medium-high heat. Add the corn with a good pinch each of salt and pepper. Return to a boil and simmer until the corn is tender, about 3 minutes. Let cool slightly, then purée the soup in batches in a blender. Strain the soup through a sieve back into the pot. Press on the solids with the back of a rubber spatula to extract as much of the flavorful purée as possible, leaving the tough corn pieces behind. Taste the soup for seasoning, adding salt and pepper to taste. Reheat over medium-low heat. If the soup is quite thick, stir in a bit more stock.

Combine the cumin and olive oil in a small saucepan and warm gently over low heat just until aromatic, 2 to 3 minutes. Set aside to cool.

Ladle the hot soup into individual bowls, drizzle the cumin oil over, and add a scattering of fresh mint. Serve right away.

serve your community while being served at Nell's!

visit www.celebratedchefs.com
www.nellsrestaurant.com

Chef Philip Mihalski

Chef and Owner Philip Mihalski's cooking approach unites his classic training in some of the most celebrated kitchens in New York City and France, with his passion for freshness and simplicity. He arrived in Seattle in the early 1990's and was a talented contributor to a number of top-rated restaurants, including Dahlia Lounge and Marco's Supperclub before opening Nell's (named for his wife) in November of 1999.

Amoré

Amoré Restaurant at the corner of 5th and Bell in Belltown, presents a unique brand of "passionately creative cuisine" and is consistently on Top Ten lists of press and online polls for *Best Italian Restaurant* in Seattle. Only fresh, organic, high-quality ingredients are used to produce a cavalcade of colors, tantalizing textures, palate-pleasers and award-winning cocktails.

Duck and Roasted Potato Salad

Serves 4

2 pounds small red or white potatoes
1 ounce dried wild mushrooms (such as porcini)
2 large duck breasts, about 1 pound each
Salt and freshly ground black pepper
4 cloves garlic, finely chopped
1/2 cup thinly sliced red onion
3 ounces oil-packed sun-dried tomatoes
10 Kalamata olives
1/4 cup dry sherry
12 ounces mixed salad greens, rinsed and dried
3 ounces feta cheese, crumbled
4 tablespoons Fig Balsamic vinegar (see below)
  or regular aged balsamic vinegar

Fig Balsamic Vinegar

4 ounces dried figs, halved
1 1/2 cups balsamic vinegar
2 tablespoons sugar
1/2 teaspoon dried red pepper flakes
2 sprigs fresh thyme
1 sprig fresh oregano
1/4 teaspoon salt
1 tablespoon olive oil

Put the potatoes in a pan of cold salted water and bring to a boil over medium-high heat. Simmer over medium heat until tender when pierced with the tip of a knife, 12 to 15 minutes. Drain and set aside. When cool, cut the potatoes into quarters. Put the dried mushrooms in a small bowl and pour hot water over to cover. Set aside to plump and soften, about 30 minutes.

Dry the duck breasts well with paper towels. Lightly score the fat side with the tip of a sharp knife without cutting into the flesh. Season the breasts with salt and pepper. Heat a large, heavy skillet over medium-high heat and add the duck breasts skin side down. Cook until the skin is lightly browned, 3 to 5 minutes. Turn the breasts and continue cooking to your taste, 3 to 5 minutes for rare to medium-rare.

Transfer the duck breasts to a cutting board and let rest while making the sauce. Drain the mushrooms, squeezing out excess water with your hands. Coarsely chop the mushrooms.

Spoon all but about 1 tablespoon of the duck fat from the skillet, then add the garlic, stirring for a few seconds, before stirring in the onions, sun-dried tomatoes, and mushrooms. Cook, stirring occasionally, until the onions are tender, 2 to 3 minutes. Cut the duck breast across into thin slices and add them to the skillet with the potatoes and olives. Stir well to evenly blend, then stir in the dry sherry and take the pan from the heat. Season to taste with salt and pepper.

For the fig balsamic vinegar, combine the figs, vinegar, sugar, thyme, oregano, pepper flakes, and salt in a

continued on page 72

serve your community while being served at Amoré!

Chef Sean Langan

Executive Chef and Owner Sean Langan's interest in Italian cuisine was piqued at an early age. He orders ingredients daily, as this is "the only way to make sure it's truly fresh". Langan roams the local markets, conceptualizing and creating his delicious, layered tastes. "I want guests to feel, understand and taste the beauty of what nature offers. Food has life – Vino, Vita, Amoré!"

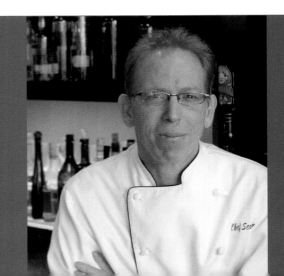

continued from page 71

medium bowl and stir well to mix. Cover and set aside in a cool place (or in the refrigerator) for 48 hours.

Discard the thyme and oregano sprigs. Transfer the figs and liquid to a food processor and pulse to purée. Strain the mixture through a fine sieve, then add the olive oil and whisk to blend. Store in an airtight container in the refrigerator.

Put the greens in the center of individual plates and spoon the duck and potato mixture over the greens. Sprinkle feta cheese over and drizzle with the fig balsamic dressing. Serve right away.

Chef's Tools

Take some simple strides forward in the way you cook at home by bringing these chef's favorite tools into your kitchen. They will give you an edge up on your skills and make your home cooking a little easier, tidier, and more efficient.

Silicone Baking Mat:

This godsend is a woven, coated thin mat that withstands high oven temperatures to ensure your treats don't stick. It works as well for any cookie, savory, or sweet, particularly those delicate items like tuiles cookies or Parmesan cheese crisps.

Immersion Blender:

This is the tool that helps bring foams to life in professional kitchens (see Modern Cooking, page 193). It's also ideal for puréeing soups and smoothing out sauces. The beauty is that you can do so right in the pan or bowl - no need to transfer to the blender container and back. The results won't be quite as silky as when using a blender, but for convenience, the immersion blender is hard to beat.

Spice Grinder:

Once you start working with whole spices and grinding them yourself, it's hard to go back to pre-ground cumin, cloves, coriander, allspice and other favorites. There are some electric grinders made with spices in mind; however, an inexpensive spare coffee grinder will work just as well.

Mandoline:

Used for slicing and cutting food, this utensil consists of two parallel working surfaces, one of which can be adjusted in height. Mandolines come in a variety of shapes, styles and sizes, all with the goal of making quick work of forming uniform slices of firm fruits and vegetables, like fennel bulb, radishes, apples, and potatoes. You can adjust for varying thicknesses, and most mandolines have julienne attachments as well.

Ricer:

This is a specialized tool that does one job particularly well. When making mashed potatoes or a recipe that uses mashed potatoes—such as potato-based gnocchi—the ricer presses the cooked potato through fine holes that create a fluffy, light mixture.

Ring Molds:

When you are served a dish that sports a lovely layering of ingredients in a perfect cylinder, its usually the result of a ring mold. This is a simple metal ring with no bottom or top. The beauty is that it allows you to layer the ingredients for your dish inside the ring, then simply lift it up to reveal an impeccable little tower of deliciousness. In a pinch, you can use an empty can that's a couple inches tall and a few inches in diameter, with both the bottom and top removed. Wrap the can well with foil and use it just as chefs do.

FLAVORFUL ACCOMPANIMENTS

What is the best part of a Thanksgiving meal? How frequently do the mashed potatoes, green beans or stuffing steal the show from the golden roasted turkey? Side dishes have this power. Designed to complement the main dish through color, flavor and texture, they have a tendency to wow the palate to such a degree that you keep going back for more.

We trust that these delightful recipes will prove to have the same scene-stealing qualities. Perhaps a few will earn a spot as a regular accompaniment to your favorite main attraction.

www.celebratedchefs.com

SIDES

Pomegranate Bistro

Consistently recognized as a premier restaurant on the Eastside, Pomegranate Bistro features a contemporary blend of Pacific Northwest cuisine and classic comfort food. Seasonal menus rotate regularly, as does the hip cocktail menu and award-winning wine list. Chef and Owner Lisa Dupar passes on her love of food through uniquely designed Northwest-infused dishes.

Heirloom Succotash with Tomato Salt

Kitchen Note: Chef Dupar uses a number of different salts from Salt Works in nearby Woodinville, their tomato salt is ideal for this recipe. You can use other flavored salts or a wonderful sea salt instead. After cutting the corn kernels from the ears, run the back of the knife over the cobs once again to remove the sweet milky corn that remains. For a richer version, replace the chicken stock with cream.

Serves 6 to 8

2 cups fresh lima beans or shelled and peeled fava beans
1 cup diced sweet onion
1 teaspoon chopped garlic
1 cup diced mixed heirloom tomatoes
4 cups freshly cut corn kernels (from about 6 ears)
1/2 cup chopped bacon
1/4 cup chicken stock or broth
1/2 teaspoon Sun Ripened Tomato Salt or other seasoned salt or sea salt
Freshly ground black pepper

Bring a large pan of salted water to a boil. Add the lima beans and cook until tender, 12 to 15 minutes. Drain well.

Heat a large skillet over medium heat. Add the bacon and cook, stirring occasionally, until the fat is rendered, 2 to 3 minutes. Add the beans, corn, tomato, onion, stock, and garlic. Season with the salt and add pepper to taste. Cook over low heat, stirring occasionally, just until the onions and corn are tender, about 5 minutes. Taste for seasoning, adding more salt or pepper to taste.

serve your community while being served at Pomegranate Bistro!

visit www.celebratedchefs.com
www.pomegranatebistro.com

Chef Lisa Dupar

Chef and Owner Lisa Dupar has been passionate about food for as long as she can remember. She grew up in Atlanta, where family gatherings centered around the kitchen and the comforting southern-style meals. This foundation, along with culinary experience in elegant European restaurants, eventually led her to become one of the Northwest's premier chefs and restaurateurs. She founded Lisa Dupar Catering in 1984, and opened Pomegranate Bistro in 2005.

emmer&rye

emmer&rye began with a vision of the connection between food and community. Eventually, that vision found a home in a 100 year-old Victorian house at the top of Queen Anne hill. Bringing together the bounty of the Northwest, skillfully-crafted dishes reflect the ingredients' true flavors and honor the seasons. Varied plate sizes offer diners the opportunity to share and savor, while creative cocktails provide a backdrop for the intersection of food and community.

Warm Emmer & Rye Salad

Kitchen Note: At emmer&rye, Chef Caswell uses namesake emmer (also known as farro) and rye grain from Bluebird Grain Farms in eastern Washington. These grains are available at many Seattle-area farmers markets. This is a versatile salad that can be served as a side dish to roasted or braised meats, or served chilled tossed with arugula and dried cherries for a wintertime salad, or with sliced radishes and asparagus in summer.

Serves 8

4 cups vegetable or chicken stock or broth
1 cup emmer or farro
1 cup rye berries
1 medium onion, finely diced
1 small fennel bulb, trimmed, cored, and finely
  diced
2 carrots, finely diced
Bouquet garni (4 parsley stems, 3 sprigs fresh thyme,
  1 fresh bay leaf tied with kitchen string)
2 tablespoons extra virgin olive oil
1/2 cup dry white wine
Kosher salt and freshly ground black pepper
Sliced radishes, for serving
Blanched or grilled asparagus, for serving

Put the stock in a small saucepan and bring just to a boil over medium-high heat; set aside.

In a deep, medium saucepan heat the olive oil over medium heat. Add the onion, fennel, and carrots with a good pinch each of salt and pepper. Cook, stirring often, until tender and lightly browned, 5 to 7 minutes. Add the emmer and rye berries and stir to evenly mix with the vegetables and lightly coat the grains with oil. Add the white wine, stirring to lift up any browned bits from the bottom of the pan. Add the bouquet garni and warm stock, stirring gently to mix. Add another pinch each of salt and pepper, cover the pan, and reduce the heat to low. Cook, stirring just occasionally, until the grains are tender but still have a bit of a bite, about 50 minutes. Remove the lid and cook until all the liquid has been absorbed by the grains, about 15 minutes longer. Taste for seasoning, adding more salt or pepper to taste.

Spoon the emmer and rye salad into individual bowls, add sliced radishes and asparagus (or other seasonal garnish), and serve right away.

serve your community while being served at emmer&rye!
visit www.celebratedchefs.com
www.emmerandrye.com

Chef Seth Caswell

Chef and Owner Seth Caswell has been cooking professionally for 18 years. After graduating from Dubrulle Culinary Arts in Vancouver, Caswell cut his teeth working in New York with such luminaries as Jean-George Vongerichten and Dan Barber. In 2005, Caswell returned to the Northwest to work with the pristine local ingredients he was so fond of. In addition to operating emmer&rye, Caswell actively serves the community through his involvement in several local food organizations.

TASTE

TASTE Restaurant, located at the Seattle Art Museum, believes in buying local ingredients directly from the producers and preparing them in seasonal dishes that comfort and dazzle. TASTE is committed to sustaining the local economy and has invested more than a million dollars in supporting local agriculture. In keeping with their mission; cuisine, conscience, community, they often feature community-farm focused dinners.

Emmer Wheat Pretzels and Dip

Kitchen Note: Look for emmer flour at some neighborhood farmers markets or on well-stocked grocery shelves with other flours and baking goods. Its nutty character adds distinctive flavor to these soft pretzels. At the restaurant, these pretzels are served with three flavorful dips. We've printed our favorite here. Visit TASTE to try the others.

Makes 15 pretzels

1/2 cup plus 2 tablespoons emmer flour
1 3/4 cups bread flour
2 tablespoons malted milk powder
2 tablespoons unsalted butter, diced
2 1/2 teaspoons kosher salt
2 ¼ teaspoons (1 envelope) active dry yeast
1 cup warm (about 105°F) water
1 1/2 teaspoons sugar
2 tablespoons baking soda
1 egg yolk
2 tablespoons Maldon sea salt or other coarse sea salt
Olive oil

Quince Dijon Dip

Makes 3/4 cup
2 ounces quince paste
1/2 cup Dijon mustard
1/2 teaspoon kosher salt

For the quince dijon dip, stir the quince paste in a small bowl to soften it. Add 2 tablespoons of the mustard and stir well to evenly blend. Stir in the remaining mustard and the salt. Refrigerate until ready to serve.

For the pretzels, combine the emmer flour, bread flour, malted milk powder, butter and salt in a medium size bowl, mix briefly and set aside. In the bowl of a stand mixer, fitted with the paddle attachment, add the yeast, sugar and water. Set aside until the yeast is frothy, about 5 minutes. Add the flour mixture into the stand mixer with the water.

Begin to mix on low speed until the dough comes together. Change from the paddle to the hook attachment, increase the speed to medium-low and knead until the dough is smooth and satiny, about 8 minutes. Lightly coat a medium bowl with olive oil and place the dough in the bowl, turning to evenly coat it in oil. Cover the bowl with a clean kitchen towel and set aside in a warm place until the dough has doubled in size, about 1 hour.

Just before the dough has finished rising, fill a large pot with water, add the baking soda, and bring to a boil over medium-high heat.

Punch down the dough and divide it into 15 equal pieces of about 1 1/2 ounces each. Roll 1 piece into a 12-inch long rope about 1/2 inch in diameter. Fold the rope in half and twist a few times, then pinch each end

continued on page 82

serve your community while being served at TASTE!

visit www.celebratedchefs.com
www.tastesam.com

Chef Lucy Damkoehler

Pastry Chef Lucy Damkoehler discovered baking at a young age when helping her father with his baking hobby. Lucy attended the New England Culinary Institute, and has worked at restaurants including Hamersley's Bistro in Boston, Gramercy Tavern in New York, and Andaluca in Seattle. Lucy says, "The best part of my job is being able to make people happy. I think desserts can bring back old memories and remind people of something mom used to make for them when they were kids".

continued from page 81

gently to secure the twist. Set aside on a lightly floured
baking sheet and cover with a clean kitchen towel.
Repeat with remaining dough. Let sit in a warm place
rise for about 30 minutes.

Preheat the oven to 325°F. Line 2 baking sheets with
silicone baking mats or parchment paper. Set 2 oven
racks on the center most positions.

Carefully add the twists to the boiling baking soda water,
3 at a time, and boil for 1 minute. Flip the twist over
and boil for 1 minute longer. Remove the twists with
tongs or a slotted spoon and place on a baking sheet to
rest. Reheat the water to a boil between batches as
needed.

Once all of the twists have been boiled, beat the egg
yolk with 2 teaspoons of water in a small dish. Brush
each twist with the egg yolk mixture and sprinkle with
sea salt. Transfer the twists to the prepared baking
sheets at least 1 inch apart. Bake until golden brown,
25 to 30 minutes, rotating the baking sheets halfway
through for even cooking.

Let the pretzel twists cool on a wire rack. Serve slightly
warm or at room temperature along with the quince
dijon dip.

Making Stock

As exemplified throughout these pages, stock is a frequent recipe ingredient. The most common is chicken stock, a good all-around choice, whether making rice or braising meat.

But many other types come up on recipes, from beef and veal to fish and lobster. The latter two, of course, are ideal used in seafood preparations such as chowder or a seafood risotto. Richer beef and veal stocks, likewise, are ideal for heartier preparations such as braised veal shanks or a meaty stew.

If time allows, a homemade stock is a preferred choice. You can tailor the recipe a bit to suit your taste and how you'll be using the recipe. And, you can make extra and freeze in 1- or 2-cup quantities, or in an ice cube tray.

The elements of a good stock are pretty basic. The "bones" of most stock are literally bones from fish or meat. Add aromatic ingredients—typically carrot, onion, celery, fresh herbs, a few peppercorns. Cover generously with cold water and you're set. Simmer time will vary with the type of stock, as little as 30 minutes for fish stock, or a few hours or more for intensely flavored beef stock. For chicken, beef, and veal, roasting the bones first in a hot oven will amplify the flavors for a richer brown stock.

Fish bones should be from a relatively mild white fish, unless you're seeking a powerful flavor, such as used when making salmon bisque. If bones aren't available, use inexpensive white fish fillets instead. The cooked fish can be used in a salad or made into cakes to pan-fry. Chop the aromatic vegetables pretty finely, so the maximum flavor will be released in the brief simmering time. Fish bones can give off bitter flavors if cooked too long - 30 minutes is usually plenty.

For chicken stock, the carcass left from last night's roasted chicken is an ideal candidate, or neck, back and wing portions from a whole chicken. Lacking that, choose inexpensive leg or thigh portions at the grocery, and save the simmered meat for another use. Two hours of gentle simmering is generally enough.

Beef and veal, lamb and rabbit stock will benefit from meaty bones, which most butchers and well-stocked meat departments at groceries have on hand. A longer cooking time is required to draw the full flavor from the bones, three to four hours. For this reason, simply quarter the vegetables rather than chop them.

For vegetable stock, use more of the aromatic vegetables and add other favorites, such as mushrooms, red bell pepper and tomato. One hour of simmering is generally sufficient.

A couple general principles with stock. Start with cold water; don't be tempted to short-cut by pouring hot water over the ingredients. And once the liquid comes to a boil, the heat should be reduced so that the stock simmers gently. Boiling will produce a cloudy stock and can become a bit bitter.

Ruth's Chris Steak House

Whether it's a romantic steak dinner for two, an important business luncheon, or a private party, Ruth's Chris Steak House can accommodate your needs. Our steakhouses provide guests with a warm, comfortable atmosphere that bolsters refined elegance and impeccable service, making your dining experience unforgettable.

Sweet Potato Casserole

Serves 8

3 pounds sweet potatoes
1 cup granulated sugar
1/2 teaspoon salt
1 teaspoon pure vanilla extract
2 eggs, well beaten
1/2 cup unsalted butter, at room temperature

Crust Mixture

1 cup packed light brown sugar
1 cup chopped pecans or other nuts (such as
   walnuts or hazelnuts)
1/3 cup all-purposes flour
3 tablespoons unsalted butter, melted

Preheat the oven to 350°F. Butter a 2-quart baking dish or individual 1-cup baking dishes.

Pierce the skin of the sweet potatoes a few times with the tip of a small knife. Bake the sweet potatoes until tender, about 1 hour. Set aside to cool, then scrape the flesh into a large bowl and mash until smooth (you should have about 3 cups purée). Add the sugar and salt and whisk to blend, then whisk in the vanilla, eggs, and butter in that order. Continue whisking to form a smooth mixture. Spoon the purée into the prepared baking dish.

For the crust, toss together the brown sugar, pecans, flour, and melted butter. Scatter this over the sweet potato base. Bake until lightly browned on top, 30 to 40 minutes. Let sit for about 15 minutes before serving.

serve your community while being served at Ruth's Chris Steak House!

visit www.celebratedchefs.com
www.ruthschris.com

Chefs Thomas Wichert & Ian Branning

Chef Branning's interest in cooking began while working at a restaurant during college. After graduating, he attended the California Culinary Academy and fine-tuned his skills, cooking across the country, before arriving in the Northwest. Chef Thomas Wichert has been working in restaurants since he was 18. In 1994, he graduated from the Culinary Institute of America. Wichert has been with RCSH for four years and is married with two young girls.

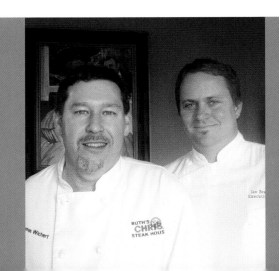

From Fresh and Salted Waters

There is no denying that seafood is a popular choice when dining out at restaurants. When you take into account just how many varieties of fish and shellfish are available from near and far, and how many different ways there are to cook seafood, it adds up to a vast array of choices.

Though chefs have resources to secure unusual species and other specialty seafoods that can be hard for home cooks to locate, you'll see that the choices in the following pages are all easy to find in well-stocked groceries and seafood markets. We think you'll be thrilled with the results of any of these selections, and that they will wow your guests.

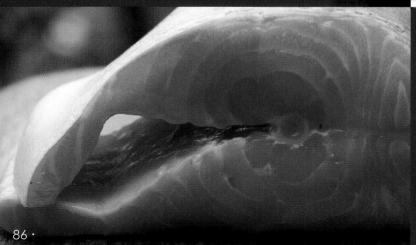

www.celebratedchefs.com

FISH AND SHELLFISH

Ray's Boathouse

A Northwest icon for over 35 years, Ray's Boathouse is world-renowned for its impeccably fresh seafood, artisan cheeses, local produce and meats, award-winning wine list featuring over 700 selections, and the spectacular bay-side view of the Olympic Mountains over Puget Sound. Featuring a rare mix of elegance and hospitality, Ray's creates an unforgettable dining experience every time.

Sablefish in Sake Kasu with Wasabi Emulsion

Kitchen Note: Look for kasu paste in Asian markets. Note that the sablefish (also known as black cod) needs to marinate for 48 hours before cooking, so plan ahead. Ideal accompaniments include steamed jasmine rice, steamed choy sum or baby bok choy, and sliced pickled ginger. You can cook the fish under the broiler rather than grilling it, if you prefer.

Serves 4

4 sablefish (black cod) fillet pieces, about 8 ounces
    each, skin on, pin bones removed
1/3 cup kosher salt, more if needed
6 ounces (about 3/4 cup) kasu paste
1/3 cup sugar
3/4 cup water
Wasabi Emulsion (see below)

Wasabi Emulsion

10 tablespoons unsalted butter, melted
3 egg yolks
2 tablespoons warm water
1 1/2 tablespoons wasabi paste
1 tablespoon rice wine vinegar
2 teaspoons chopped pickled ginger
Kosher salt

Lay the black cod fillets in a single layer in a glass baking dish. Sprinkle a generous layer of salt over the fish, cover the dish with plastic wrap, and refrigerate for 24 hours.

Rinse the salt from the fish and pat dry. Clean out and dry the baking dish and return the fish fillets to the dish.

Beat the kasu paste with the sugar using a whisk or electric mixer. When the paste is smooth, slowly add the water, whisking to evenly blend. Pour the kasu mixture evenly over the fish, cover the dish with plastic wrap, and refrigerate for another 24 hours.

Shortly before serving, preheat an outdoor grill.

Lift the sablefish fillets from the marinade, allowing excess to drip off. Grill the fish until nicely browned on the surface and just opaque through the thickest part, 3 to 5 minutes per side depending on the thickness of the fish.

For the Wasabi Emulsion, combine the egg yolks, water, wasabi paste, vinegar, and ginger in a blender. With the blades running, slowly add the warm melted butter. Blend until fully incorporated and emulsified. Transfer to a bowl and season to taste with salt.

Transfer the grilled sablefish to individual plates, spoon the wasabi emulsion over, and serve.

Chef Peter Birk

Executive Chef Peter Birk's skill for classically based preparations with modern twists is a perfect match to the versatility and variety of seafood that Ray's offers. He is an early-morning regular at the Ballard Sunday Farmers Market and an authority on artisan cheeses, fresh shellfish and crustaceans, sustainability, wild salmon, and grass-fed beef.

Tulio

Step through the antique revolving doors of Tulio Ristorante in the heart of downtown Seattle and it's as if you've entered a bustling Italian trattoria. Chef Walter Pisano's boldly-flavored dishes are both simple and sophisticated, combining rustic Italian preparations with fresh Pacific Northwest ingredients. It's easy to understand why Tulio is widely regarded as one of the city's best restaurants.

Venetian-Style Mussels

Serves 4 to 6

1 tablespoon olive oil
1 clove garlic, halved
3 pounds live mussels, scrubbed and debearded
5 ripe tomatoes, about 1 1/2 pounds, peeled, seeded, and finely diced
1/4 cup brandy
1 teaspoon finely grated lemon zest
1/2 cup slivered fresh basil
3 tablespoons chopped fresh flat-leaf parsley
1/2 teaspoon dried red pepper flakes

Heat the oil in a large saucepan over medium heat. Add the garlic and cook until it turns golden brown, 2 to 3 minutes, stirring occasionally. Add the mussels and stir constantly for 1 to 2 minutes, then cover the pan. Cook until the mussels have opened, 5 to 7 minutes, gently shaking the pan every few minutes. Use a slotted spoon to lift out the mussels to a large bowl and set aside. If the mussels have given off quite a lot of liquid, boil the cooking liquids to reduce to a few tablespoons.

Add the tomatoes, brandy, and lemon zest to the pan. Cover and cook for another 2 minutes. Remove the lid and gently stir in the basil, parsley, and pepper flakes.

To serve, remove half of each mussel shell. Place the mussels on the half shell on a platter and spoon the sauce from the pan over the top. Serve immediately.

serve your community while being
served at Tulio!

visit www.celebratedchefs.com
www.tulio.com

Chef Walter Pisano

For Chef Walter Pisano, running an Italian restaurant seemed preordained. As the son of an East Coast Italian restaurateur, the business runs in his blood. Through apprenticeships, Pisano was trained in classical European cuisine. He came to Seattle to help open The Hunt Club, then took a culinary tour of Europe, immersing in the cuisines of France and Italy. Opened in 1992, Tulio, named for his father, showcases Chef Pisano's Italian roots.

Pearl

Pearl Bar & Dining is the urban, go-to gathering spot in the hottest entertainment venue on the Eastside: Lincoln Square. The contemporary Northwest menu changes frequently to showcase fresh, seasonal and local products. Pearl also features handcrafted signature cocktails, a vast selection of premium wine and beer alongside gracious service. From a light lunch to an elegant dinner with friends, Pearl has options to suit every occasion.

Halibut with Grilled Prawns, Heirloom Tomato Salad and Harissa Vinaigrette

Kitchen Note: A couple of summery seasonal accompaniments for this halibut recipe include a simple tabbouleh salad or steamed fresh sweet corn.

Serves 4

1 pound mixed heirloom tomatoes
1 to 2 tablespoons basil oil or extra virgin olive oil
Kosher salt and freshly ground black pepper
4 halibut fillet pieces, about 6 ounces each
8 medium shrimp, peeled and deveined
2 to 3 tablespoons olive oil
1 cup Harissa Vinaigrette (see below)
Fresh basil leaves, for garnish

Harissa Vinaigrette

1/4 cup freshly squeezed lemon juice
2 tablespoons minced garlic
2 tablespoons minced fresh cilantro
1 tablespoon red chile powder, or to taste
1 tablespoon ground cumin
1 teaspoon cayenne pepper, or to taste
1 teaspoon kosher salt
1/2 cup olive oil

Begin with the vinaigrette. Whisk together the lemon juice, garlic, cilantro, chile powder, cumin, cayenne, and salt until well blended. Slowly add the olive oil, whisking constantly. Taste for seasoning, adding more chile or salt to taste. Set aside.

For the salad, thinly slice the tomatoes and arrange them as a base on individual plates. Drizzle with a bit of the basil oil and season lightly with salt and pepper.

Preheat an outdoor grill.

Rub the halibut pieces and the shrimp with the olive oil and season with salt and pepper. Thread the shrimp onto a metal or soaked bamboo skewer for easier handling on the grill. Grill the halibut until just a touch of translucence remains in the center, 3 to 4 minutes per side depending on the thickness of the fish. Grill the shrimp alongside the halibut until just evenly opaque, about 2 minutes per side.

Set the grilled halibut on top of the tomatoes. Remove the shrimp from the skewers and place 2 on top of each piece of halibut. Drizzle the harissa vinaigrette over and serve, garnishing each plate with a basil leaf.

Chef Bradley Dickinson

Pearl marks the next chapter in life for Executive Chef and Partner Bradley Dickinson. From kitchen operations to team development, menu creation to restaurant design, Chef Dickinson has over 20 years of experience. A Seattle native, Chef Dickinson, draws inspiration from emerging culinary trends and the cultivation of his home vegetable garden. He also enjoys using his chef skills to lend support to the community.

photo courtesy of Rina Jordan Photography

stumbling Goat Bistro

The Stumbling Goat Bistro is a neighborhood restaurant that features seasonal ingredients from local growers, farms, and foragers. We offer a small but varied wine list, as well as a full bar and innovative cocktail menu. Our menu highlights the best that the Pacific Northwest has to offer, with an emphasis on incorporating seasonal foods into our small plates, entrees, desserts, and cocktails.

Pan Seared Salmon with Anise Glazed Beets

Serves 2

1 tablespoon vegetable oil
2 salmon fillet pieces, about 6 ounces each, skin and pin bones removed
2 tablespoons extra virgin olive oil
2 cups lightly packed wild or hydroponic watercress, rinsed, dried, and trimmed
1 small fennel bulb, trimmed, halved, cored, and very thinly sliced
Freshly squeezed juice of 1 lemon

Anise Glazed Beets

1 large or 2 medium red beets, about 8 ounces total, trimmed
1 cup sugar
1/2 cup champagne or white wine vinegar
1/2 cup water
2 teaspoons anise seeds or fennel seeds

Put the beets in a pan of cold salted water and bring to a boil. Reduce the heat to medium and simmer until the beets are tender when pierced with the tip of a knife, 50 to 60 minutes. The beets should be covered with water throughout; add more hot water to the pan as needed. Drain and let cool, then peel away the skin with your fingers. Set aside.

Combine the sugar, vinegar, water, and anise seeds in a medium saucepan. Bring to a boil over medium-high heat, stirring to help the sugar dissolve. Reduce the heat to medium-low and simmer the mixture until reduced to a thick syrup, about 20 minutes. Strain the syrup into a medium bowl. Cut the beets into 1/4 inch thick slices and add them to the syrup, stirring gently to evenly coat the slices.

Heat the vegetable oil in a medium skillet over medium-high heat. Add the salmon and cook until nicely browned on both sides and just a touch of translucence remains in the middle, 2 to 3 minutes per side.

Arrange the beet slices in a pile in the center of each plate. Drizzle 1 tablespoon of the extra virgin olive oil around. Set the salmon on top of the beets and drizzle some of the beet syrup around, adding a few drops to the olive oil so that it beads up. Combine the watercress and fennel in a medium bowl, add the remaining 1 tablespoon of the olive oil and the lemon juice. Toss to mix and add to the plates alongside the salmon.

serve your community while being served at Stumbling Goat Bistro!

visit www.celebratedchefs.com
www.stumblinggoatbistro.com

Chef Joshua Theilen

Joshua Theilen has worked in some of Seattle's top restaurants and catering establishments since graduating from the Art Institute of Seattle in 1999, including the Hunt Club, Restaurant Zoë, and Lowell Hunt Premier Catering. Most recently, Joshua was the executive sous chef at Trellis, where he won the *Northwest Stir 2008 Young Lion – Sous Chef* award. Chef Theilen brings a passion for clean flavors, fresh local product and classic technique.

Fresh Bistro

Fresh Bistro features a seasonally-inspired menu, using ingredients from local producers and offering a fresh take on classic bistro-style dishes. A favorite for casual dining and romantic evenings, Chef Dalis Chea's menu showcases a variety of flavorful selections for every palate. Diners can enjoy brunch, lunch, dinner and happy hour, indoor/outdoor seating, and a space for private parties.

Citrus Miso Glazed Black Cod with Orange and Fennel Salad

Kitchen Note: Red miso paste is a thick blend of fermented soy beans used in a wide range of Japanese recipes. You can find it in the refrigerated section of Asian markets and well-stocked groceries. You can use halibut or salmon in place of the black cod; whatever fish you use, choose the freshest available.

Serves 6

1/3 cup soy sauce
1/3 cup sugar
1/3 cup fresh squeezed orange juice
2 tablespoons red miso paste
1/4 teaspoon freshly ground black pepper
6 black cod fillet pieces, skin and pin bones removed, about 5 ounces each

Orange and Fennel Salad

Segments of 3 oranges (see page 153)
Juice and grated zest of 1 orange
1 small fennel bulb, trimmed, cored, and very thinly sliced
1/2 cup pickled red onion or 1/4 cup thinly sliced fresh red onion
1/4 cup chervil leaves or small leaves flat-leaf parsley

Citrus Vinaigrette

1/4 cup olive oil
1 tablespoon freshly squeezed orange juice
1 tablespoon rice wine vinegar
Salt and freshly ground black pepper

Stir together the soy sauce, sugar, orange juice, miso, and black pepper in a small bowl until the sugar is dissolved. Put the fish pieces in a large resealable plastic bag and pour the miso mixture over. Seal the bag and marinate in the refrigerator for at least 3 hours.

Shortly before serving, preheat the oven to 350°F. Line a rimmed baking sheet with parchment paper or foil and lightly oil it.

Lift the fish pieces from the miso marinade, allowing excess to drip off, and arrange them on the baking sheet. Bake until firm to the touch and lightly browned, 12 to 15 minutes.

For the salad, combine the orange segments, orange juice and zest, fennel, red onion, and chervil in a medium bowl. For the vinaigrette, whisk together the olive oil, vinegar, and orange juice with salt and pepper to taste. Pour the dressing over the orange mixture and toss to mix. Taste for seasoning, adding more salt or pepper to taste.

Transfer the fish to warmed individual plates and top the fillets with some of the orange and fennel salad. Serve right away.

serve your community while being served at Fresh Bistro!

visit www.celebratedchefs.com
www.freshbistroseattle.com

Chef Dalis Chea

Dalis (pronounced 'Dally') Chea is the Executive Chef and co-owner of Fresh Bistro, an internationally-inspired bistro-style restaurant in West Seattle. Also the Executive Chef for award-winning local caterer Herban Feast, Dalis' menu's feature seasonal, locally sourced ingredients to produce interesting, flavorful dishes. Dalis graduated from Le Cordon Bleu Culinary Arts Program in Portland.

salish Lodge & spa

Salish Lodge & Spa is a serene and picturesque retreat. Enjoy the hush of the misting falls, clink of toasting glasses and a feast of Chef Jack Strong's indigenous Northwest cuisine. The Dining Room maintains a commitment to food ethics, while preparing dishes with uncompromising flavor compositions. At Salish Lodge & Spa, the fare not only tastes good but is selected with Mother Nature in mind.

Steelhead with Butternut Squash Hash

Kitchen Note: If steelhead is unavailable, you could use salmon, halibut, or black cod fillets instead. Chef Jack Strong smokes belly portions from steelhead fillets to flake and add to the butternut squash hash. You can use a bit of top-quality hot smoked salmon, flaked, or simply omit the fish from the accompanying hash. Russet potatoes are a fine substitution for the purple potatoes. At the Salish, this dish is finished with a drizzle of lightly sweetened reduction of red wine and port for an extra flourish.

Serves 4

4 steelhead fillet pieces, about 6 ounces each, skin on, pin bones removed
2 teaspoons olive oil
1/2 teaspoon kosher salt
1 tablespoon unsalted butter
1/2 teaspoon thinly sliced chives
4 tablespoons Lemon Thyme Butter (see below)

Butternut Squash Hash

1/4 cup olive oil
1 small onion, diced
1 cup diced butternut squash
1 cup diced purple potatoes or russet potatoes
1/4 cup thinly sliced chives
2 teaspoons minced garlic
1 teaspoon minced fresh thyme
Kosher salt and freshly ground black pepper

Lemon-Thyme Butter

1/2 cup unsalted butter, at room temperature
1 teaspoon finely chopped thyme
1 teaspoon finely grated lemon zest

Preheat an outdoor grill.

Brush the flesh sides of the steelhead fillets with 1 teaspoon of the olive oil and season lightly with salt and pepper. Set the fillets on the grill skin side down and grill for 2 minutes. Carefully lift the fillets and rotate them 90 degrees, setting them back skin side down (this makes a crosshatch pattern on the skin). Cook for another 2 minutes. Turn the fillets over and cook another 2 minutes. Again lift the fillet and rotate 90 degrees, then continue grilling until just a touch of translucence remains in the thickest part of the fish, 1 to 2 minutes longer. (For thick fillet pieces you may want to add an extra minute or two to each side.)

Melt the butter in a large skillet over medium heat. Add the hash and toss until lightly browned and heated through, 2 to 3 minutes.

continued on page 100

serve your community while being served at salish Lodge & spa!
visit www.celebratedchefs.com
www.salishlodge.com

Chef Jack Strong

Chef Jack Strong brings nearly 20 years of experience to The Dining Room at Salish Lodge & Spa. Hailing from the Confederated Tribes of the Siletz, Jack's heritage plays a strong role in his culinary philosophy. A graduate of the culinary program at Lane Community College, Strong has honed his skills at highly-acclaimed restaurants up and down the West Coast. Chef Strong leverages farm-fresh, native ingredients of the region to develop indigenous Northwest cuisine.

continued from page 99

For the hash, heat the olive oil in a large skillet over medium-high heat. Add the onion and cook, stirring often, until tender and lightly browned, 2 to 3 minutes. Add the squash and potatoes and stir to evenly mix with the onion. Cook over medium heat, stirring often, until the potatoes and squash are nearly tender but still holding their shape, about 10 minutes. Add the chives, garlic, and thyme, with salt and pepper to taste. Set aside, or cool and refrigerate if making in advance.

For the lemon-thyme butter, stir together the butter, lemon zest, and thyme in a small bowl until thoroughly blended. Set aside until needed, or refrigerate if making in advance.

Spoon the warm hash just to one side of center on individual plates and lay the grilled steelhead over the hash. Top each fillet with 1 tablespoon of the lemon thyme butter, sprinkle the chives over the fish, and serve.

Northwest Seafood

Seafood in Seattle brings to mind fish flying at the Pike Place Market, oysters on the half-shell, alder-planked salmon, steamed clams. It can seem almost cliché, but the delicious truth is that seafood is very much a part of the fabric of our region. Family traditions here are built around picking oysters on the shores of Hood Canal, heading to Westport to go razor clam digging, taking crab pots to the beachfront cabin on Whidbey Island for a summertime of Dungeness feasts.

Seattle area restaurants reflect that tradition in spades. Not only do seafood-centric restaurants abound - Ray's Boathouse (page 88), Seastar (page 14) and Shucker's (page 60) - but you're pretty well guaranteed of finding a decent selection on many menus around town. And while you'll find lobster, striped bass, and other "out of town" options, many chefs trumpet the products of the region by showcasing local seafoods.

Some varieties you'll find in this volume include albacore tuna, a wonderful variety that hasn't received much attention with ahi so much in the limelight. But ahi is facing some sustainability challenges, and many chefs are looking to alternatives such as albacore, which is caught (and carefully monitored) in the Pacific waters off the Washington and Oregon coast.

Another local favorite is black cod, which also goes by "sablefish". Although not actually a member of the family, it does have white flaky flesh akin to cod. Black cod is much richer, a lush fish that's often prepared simply - grilled or pan-seared. A traditional Northwest preparation is "kasu" black cod, which has been cured with sugar and salt, then marinated in kasu (sake lees, the paste that remains at the end of the sake-making process) before grilling. Ray's Boathouse has served it for about three decades, and shares the recipe with us (see page 88).

We could write volumes (and some have!) about the salmon. There's no underestimating how much this fish means, especially to the native people of the Northwest, but also to every generation since. Alder-grilled or smoked, chowdered or pickled, roasted whole or cured raw for gravlax - salmon is a showpiece on both home and restaurant tables.

Clams and mussels are ubiquitous in Seattle, from the casual fare of a neighborhood brewpub to the more refined white-tablecloth destinations. Steamed with beer, white wine or fish broth, accented with onions, Thai curry or chorizo sausage, the manifestations of these favorite shellfish are countless.

And oysters - this region's most beloved bivalve. Purists will only eat them freshly shucked, with no adornment, preferably plucked moments earlier from a pristine Northwest beach. But those oyster beds are so delightfully close to this city's restaurant kitchens that even if we're not standing beside the lapping tide, we have ample opportunity to indulge. Those who do eat oysters cooked often still opt for simple preparations, like grilled over live coals, roasted with an herb-crumb topping or warmed in cream for an elegant oyster stew.

il Bistro

Tucked away beneath the Pike Place Market, il Bistro has been a Seattle favorite for more than 30 years, providing authentic Italian cuisine with an intimate ambiance. Like a candlelit restaurant nestled in the foothills of Tuscany, il Bistro provides fresh-from-the-market ingredients and a romantic ambiance along a cobblestone street. It is an ideal setting for a perfect evening.

Cioppino

Kitchen Note: An ideal accompaniment to this dish would be thick slices of Tuscan bread that have been brushed with olive oil and crushed garlic, then grilled or broiled.

Serves 4

1/4 cup olive oil
1 yellow bell pepper, cored, seeded, and finely
  diced
1/2 cup finely diced sweet onion
2 tablespoons minced garlic
1 pound live mussels, scrubbed and debearded
1 pound live Manila or other hard-shell clams, rinsed
1 cooked Dungeness crab, about 2 pounds,
  cleaned and quartered, shells lightly cracked
8 ounces salmon, skin and pin bones removed, cut
  into 1-inch pieces
8 large prawns, shelled and deveined
8 ounces calamari rings and tentacles
2 tablespoons slivered fresh basil
3 cups marinara sauce
  (homemade or top quality prepared)
1 cup dry white wine
1/4 cup freshly squeezed lemon juice
Salt and freshly ground black pepper
Extra virgin olive oil, for serving
Lemon slices, for serving

Heat 2 tablespoons of the olive oil in a large deep sauté pan or pot over medium heat. Add the bell pepper, onion, and garlic and cook, stirring, until the onions are translucent, 3 to 5 minutes. Add the mussels and clams. Cover the pan and cook just until the mussels and clams have opened, 4 to 5 minutes. Shake the pan gently once or twice during cooking.

Add the marinara sauce, white wine, and lemon juice and bring just to a low boil. Add the salmon, prawns, and crab, cover, and cook for 3 to 4 minutes longer. Season the cioppino to taste with salt and pepper. Add the calamari and basil, stirring them gently into the mixture. Cook just until the calamari is opaque, 1 to 2 minutes.

Distribute the seafood evenly among 4 large shallow bowls, setting the Dungeness crab portions on top in the center. Ladle the broth over the seafood, drizzle with a bit of extra virgin olive oil, and add a lemon slice alongside.

serve your community while being served at il Bistro!
visit www.celebratedchefs.com
www.ilbistro.net

Chef Nathan Luoma

Executive Chef Nathan Luoma has an extensive background of world travel, Italian, Spanish and New World cuisine. He happily prepares il Bistro's signature dishes; many of which have been on the menu for 35 years, alongside his own creations, using many of the local ingredients found right outside his kitchen door in the Pike Place Market.

SkyCity at the Needle

SkyCity at the Needle welcomes guests with stunning views and a passion for food, wine, and exceptional service. Your experience begins with a 500-foot journey to the restaurant that revolves 360° in the sky, providing unparalleled views of the city and beyond. Culinary offerings include seafood harvested from Pacific Northwest waters, fresh produce and meat grown by Washington farmers, and an award-winning list of Northwest wines.

Grilled Wild King Salmon with Smoky Bacon and Crab Fondue

Kitchen Note: This dish is simple to prepare, using simple ingredients. At SkyCity at the Needle, the salmon is often served with a morel mushroom flan. Sautéed mushrooms would be an easy alternative to serve here.

Serves 4

4 wild king salmon fillet pieces, about 8 ounces each, skin and pin bones removed
1 tablespoon olive oil

Smoky Bacon and Crab Fondue

4 ounces thinly sliced bacon, cut into 1/4 inch pieces
1 medium leek, split, cleaned, and thinly sliced
2 tablespoons unsalted butter
3 tablespoons all-purpose flour
1 cup whole milk, more if needed
1/2 cup whipping cream
5 ounces Dungeness crab meat
Juice of 1 lemon
1 teaspoon minced fresh thyme
Salt and freshly ground black pepper

For the smoky bacon and crab fondue, cook the bacon in a medium saucepan over medium heat until crispy, stirring occasionally, about 10 minutes. Drain off all but about 1 tablespoon of the fat from the pan, then add the leek and cook, stirring often, until tender and translucent, 2 to 3 minutes. Add the butter and stir until melted, then add the flour and stir well to evenly blend. Cook, stirring often, for 2 to 3 minutes. Slowly add the milk, stirring constantly, followed by the cream. Reduce the heat to medium-low and cook, stirring often, until the sauce thickens, about 5 minutes. Pick over the crab meat to remove any bits of shell or cartilage. Take the pan from the heat and add the crab, lemon juice, and thyme with salt and pepper to taste. Keep warm over very low heat while cooking the salmon.

Preheat an outdoor grill to high heat. Rub the salmon with the oil and season generously with salt and pepper. Grill the fish until just a touch of translucence remains in the center, 3 to 4 minutes per side. You can turn the fish 45 degrees in its position on the grill if you'd like to make a cross-hatch grill mark pattern on the surface.

Arrange the salmon pieces on individual plates. If the sauce has become quite thick, stir in a bit more milk and warm through. Spoon the sauce over the salmon and serve.

serve your community while being served at skyCity at the Needle!

visit www.celebratedchefs.com
www.spaceneedle.com

Chef Jeff Maxfield

Line cook, sous chef, chef de cuisine, and Executive Chef are just a few of the roles Jeff Maxfield has held at notable restaurants in Seattle, Hawaii, and Arizona. At Canlis, he developed a passion for all things Northwest, and he brings that same fervor to SkyCity. Executive Chef Maxfield has a knack for bringing local flavors and ingredients together to make one-of-a-kind dishes. This high-altitude dining experience is enhanced by Maxfield's culinary creativity.

Russell's

Nestled in a beautifully restored farmhouse in Bothell, Russell's provides an exceptional dining experience, a notable wine list, and the drive to deliver a simple menu showcasing plenty of options for the Northwest food lover. Russell's also gives you the opportunity to enjoy the work of one of Seattle's most sought after catering companies, Russell Lowell Catering, any time you like.

Pan Seared Halibut with Cherry and Poblano Salsa

Serves 4

4 halibut fillet pieces, about 6 ounces each
Salt and freshly ground black pepper
2 tablespoons olive oil

Cherry and Poblano Salsa

2 tablespoons canola oil
1 cup diced cipollini onions
1 cup pitted fresh sweet cherries
   (such as Bing or Rainier)
1/2 cup minced yellow bell pepper
1/2 cup roasted, seeded, and diced poblano chiles
2 tablespoons honey
1 tablespoon chopped fresh flat-leaf parsley
2 teaspoons freshly squeezed lemon juice,
   more if needed
Kosher salt

For the salsa, heat the oil in a medium skillet over medium heat. Add the onions and cook, stirring occasionally, until tender and translucent, 3 to 5 minutes. Set aside to cool.

Put the cooled onions in a medium bowl and add the cherries, yellow bell pepper, roasted poblano, honey, parsley, and lemon juice with a good pinch of salt. Stir to evenly mix and set aside for 30 minutes to allow the flavors to meld. Taste the salsa again, adding more salt or lemon juice to taste.

Preheat the oven to 400 F.

Season the halibut fillets with salt and pepper. Heat the olive oil in a large ovenproof skillet, preferably nonstick, over medium-high heat. Add the halibut fillets and brown well on the bottom, 2 to 3 minutes. Transfer the halibut to the oven and roast until just a touch of translucence remains at the center of the thickest part, 4 to 8 minutes longer, depending on the thickness of the fish.

Transfer the halibut to individual plates, spoon the cherry and poblano salsa over, and serve.

serve your community while being served at Russell's!

visit www.celebratedchefs.com
www.rdlcatering.com

Chef Russell Lowell

Chef Lowell began his culinary career at age 15. Extensive travel and cooking, led Lowell to Executive Chef roles in several well-known restaurants across the nation. In 2007, Russell's was selected to host the prestigious *James Beard Foundation's Taste America* celebration. Executive Chef Lowell's reverence for life and cuisine, complemented by his drive to deliver an exceptional experience, makes him one of the Pacific Northwest's most respected chefs.

photo courtesy of Daphne Taylor - Creative Image Photography

Eva Restaurant

Owners James Hondros and Amy McCray welcome you to Eva, a casual, neighborhood restaurant offering fine dining in a relaxed atmosphere. The restaurant features West Coast modern cuisine, focusing on local produce and natural meats. James Hondros brings a strong wine background and has compiled an eclectic, rationally-priced wine list dedicated to the idea that wine is an integral part of a good meal and not solely an accessory of the connoisseur.

Albacore Tuna with Fingerling Potatoes, Chorizo, Shaved Garlic, and Aleppo Oil

Kitchen Note: Aleppo is a type of chile pepper from Syria, most commonly available in dried ground form. It has a moderate heat level and a complex flavor that can be a bit fruity, spicy, and even salty tasting. Look for it in specialty spice shops or well-stocked gourmet stores. In its place you can use dried red pepper flakes, but they will be a bit hotter.

Serves 4

1/2 pound fingerling potatoes
16 large cloves garlic, thinly sliced
1/2 cup olive oil
2 teaspoons dried Aleppo pepper
8 ounces Spanish cured chorizo
1 pint cherry tomatoes, halved if large
4 albacore tuna steaks, about 5 ounces each
Salt and freshly ground black pepper
1 tablespoon canola oil
1 bunch watercress, stemmed, rinsed, and dried
3/4 cup oil-cured olives
Juice of 1 lemon

Preheat the oven to 400°F.

Put the potatoes in a large pan of cold salted water. Bring to a boil over medium-high heat, then reduce the heat to medium and simmer until tender when pierced with the tip of a knife, 15 to 20 minutes. Drain and let cool.

Combine the garlic and 1/4 cup of the olive oil in a small skillet. Warm over medium-high heat until the oil just begins to bubble at the edges. Reduce the heat to low and cook gently until the garlic is tender, about 15 minutes. Strain the oil into a small bowl, reserving the garlic as well.

Combine the remaining 1/4 cup of the olive oil with the Aleppo pepper and warm over low heat. When the oil is just warmed, set it aside to steep for 30 minutes. Strain the oil through a fine sieve lines with paper towel or a coffee filter into a small bowl (it may take a few minutes to drip through), discarding the pepper.

Remove the casing from the chorizo and cut into 1-inch pieces. Halve the fingerling potatoes lengthwise. Heat a large, ovenproof sauté pan or skillet over medium-high heat. Coat the hot pan with 1 tablespoon of the garlic oil and carefully arrange the potatoes cut side down in the pan. Roast the potatoes in the oven until golden brown, 12 to 15 minutes. Add the chorizo and cherry tomatoes and roast until warmed, 5 to 7 minutes longer.

Meanwhile, season the tuna with salt and pepper. Heat a large sauté pan or skillet over high heat. Add the canola

continued on page 110

serve your community while being served at Eva!

Chef Amy McCray

As a college graduation gift, Chef Amy McCray's father gave her a spatula for flipping burgers—which he thought to be the perfect match for her English literature degree. Inspired by the challenge, Amy went to cooking school where she met her future husband, James Hondros. After stints as sous chef at the Dahlia Lounge and chef at Chez Shea, Amy and James opened Eva in 2001.

continued from page 109

oil, and when the oil is hot carefully add the tuna. Sear for 1 minute on each side. Set the fish aside on a plate to avoid overcooking.

Combine the watercress and olives in a large bowl and add the still-warm potato mixture and the cooked garlic. Drizzle with lemon juice, the remaining garlic oil, and a pinch each of salt and pepper. Toss well to mix. Arrange the salad on individual plates. Cut each tuna steak into slices and fan them out over the salad. Drizzle the Aleppo oil over and serve.

Pike Place Market

With the ever-growing number of neighborhood and regional farmers markets that are popping up around the country, the cook - both professional and amateur - is increasingly blessed with opportunities to stock his or her kitchen with really fresh, very local foods. It gives us all a chance to shop a bit more like a chef, who often has access to unusual products and hyper-seasonal items that rarely make it into our standard grocery stores.

We are extra fortunate that the oldest continually-operating farmers market in the country, the 103+ year-old Pike Place Market, calls the Emerald City home. It serves as a touchstone for the valuable connection that can be made between bustling urbanites and rural farmlands, ensuring that regional agriculture traditions continue and flourish for years to come.

Generations of Seattleites have fed culinary inspiration for the inevitable "what's for dinner" question by strolling through the Market. All you need do is to cast your eyes over offerings at the low stalls to the north end of the Market, where farmers show up daily with whatever's been harvested in the past 24 hours or so - spring sweet onions, local corn, delicate berries, vibrant chile peppers, mounds of delicious greens.

With your canvas shopping bags filled with local produce, it's time to hit one of the many cheese vendors, scan the offerings at an old-fashioned butcher counter, scope out the seafood piled high on mounds of ice, pick up a loaf of bread, and maybe choose a bottle of Washington wine at Pike & Western Wine Shop. Consider locally-made sausage or delicate quails' eggs, regional honey or local hazelnuts. In no time, you'll have the fixings for a meal (or two or three) that showcases our area by way of the regional market products.

Even the most locally-oriented chefs, though, don't live by fiddlehead ferns and wild foraged mushrooms alone! We can eat locally but with a global palate by melding regional offerings with flavors from all parts of the world. The Pike Place Market comes through with everything from distinctive, exotic spices to Latin American foods, exquisite olive oils to outstanding teas and coffees, among many other selections that add variety to the dinnertime menu.

It's fun and inspiring to step out of our everyday shopping routines and make a trip to the Pike Place Market now and then. And you can even fuel your shopping time with a steaming cup of coffee and pastry, or lunch or dinner at a number of great restaurants that support Celebrated Chefs!

Maximilien

Maximilien is a romantic and charming French restaurant located in Pike Place Market. It harbors all the old-world charm of any hideaway in Paris. Inside, you are greeted by a panorama that takes in the Puget Sound, West Seattle, and the Olympic Mountains, all framed by huge picture windows. The food is as spectacular as the view, making Maximilien one of Seattle's most sought after dining destinations for more than 30 years.

Grilled Wild Salmon and Warm Butter Lettuce Salad

Serves 2

1/2 pound fingerling potatoes, peeled
3 teaspoons extra virgin olive oil
1/2 cup thinly sliced red onion
8 red cherry tomatoes, halved if large
1/2 cup chopped, toasted walnuts (see page 153)
Salt and freshly ground black pepper
2 wild salmon fillet pieces, about 5 ounces each
1 head butter lettuce, leaves separated, rinsed,
   and dried, large leaves torn
1 tablespoon balsamic vinegar, more to taste
2 tablespoons chopped chives, for serving

Put the potatoes in a medium pan of cold salted water. Bring the water to a boil over medium-high heat, then reduce the heat to medium and simmer until the potatoes are tender when pierced with the tip of a knife, 12 to 15 minutes. Drain and let cool slightly, then halve the potatoes lengthwise.

Preheat an outdoor grill to high heat.

Meanwhile, heat 2 teaspoons of the olive oil in a large skillet over medium heat. Add the potatoes and brown lightly, about 5 minutes. Add the onion, tomatoes, and walnuts and cook, stirring occasionally, until the onions are tender and aromatic, 3 to 5 minutes longer. Season to taste with salt and pepper; set aside while cooking the salmon.

Rub the salmon pieces with 1 teaspoon of the olive oil and season with salt and pepper. Grill until nicely browned on the surface and just a bit translucent in the center, 2 to 4 minutes per side.

Reheat the potato mixture over medium-high heat. Add the greens and vinegar to the skillet and cook, stirring, until the greens are just warmed but still crunchy, about 30 seconds. Arrange the vegetable mixture in the center of individual plates, top with the salmon fillets, and sprinkle the chives over. Drizzle any pan juices around the fish and serve.

serve your community while being served at Maximilien!

visit www.celebratedchefs.com
www.maximilienrestaurant.com

Chef Christian Potvin

Executive Chef Christian Potvin began as a 16-year-old apprentice in Le Meaban in France. He moved to New York City to work at Café des Artistes, and then at the acclaimed five-star La Vieille Maison in Boca Raton, Florida. Chef Potvin moved to Seattle in 2000, working at Au Bouchon before joining Maximilien in 2004.

Place Pigalle

Charming and clandestine, Place Pigalle combines the flavor, spirit, and soul of Pike Place Market with cozy quarters, stunning views, and seasonal menus full of local ingredients. With the award-winning wine list and a bar specializing in the unusual, Owners Seth and Lluvia Walker, along with Chef Tom Schultz, invite you to Place Pigalle to relive a bit of Seattle's intriguing history.

Seared Scallops with Pancetta and Brussels Sprouts Hash and Prosecco Beurre Blanc

Kitchen Note: Try to find "dry pack" or "natural" scallops that have not been plumped up; they will sear more easily and not put out as much liquid as they cook.

Serves 2

6 to 8 large sea scallops, about 1 pound
Salt and freshly ground black pepper
2 tablespoons olive oil
1 teaspoon unsalted butter
1 pound Brussels sprouts, trimmed and thinly sliced

Pancetta Gastrique

4 ounces pancetta, finely diced
1/2 cup apple cider vinegar
1/4 cup sugar
1 tablespoon pure maple syrup
1 tablespoon stone ground mustard

Prosecco Beurre Blanc

1/2 cup prosecco or other dry sparkling wine
1 small shallot, julienned
2 tablespoons whipping cream
4 to 6 tablespoons unsalted butter, cut into 1/2-inch cubes and chilled

For the gastrique, cook the pancetta in a medium skillet over medium heat until lightly browned and crisp, about 5 minutes. Do not drain the fat. Add the vinegar and stir to loosen any cooked bits from the bottom of the skillet. Add the sugar and stir to help the sugar dissolve. Bring to a boil, and simmer until the liquid is reduced by one third, about 5 minutes. Take the pan from the heat and

stir in the maple syrup and mustard. Set aside.

For the beurre blanc, combine the proscecco, shallot, and cream in a small sauce pan over medium heat. Bring to a simmer and cook it until the liquid has reduced by two thirds. Take the pan from the heat and whisk in the butter 1 or 2 cubes at a time, whisking to fully melt and incorporate each addition before adding the next. Warm the pan for a few moments on low heat if needed. Once all the butter has been incorporated, season lightly with salt and set aside.

Pat the scallops dry with paper towels and season them with salt and pepper. Heat a sauté pan or skillet over medium-high heat and add 1 tablespoon of the olive oil and the butter. When the oil is lightly smoking, add the scallops and sear until lightly browned, 1 to 2 minutes. Turn the scallops and sear on the second side for 1 minute (if your pan is quite heavy and holds its heat well, there may be enough heat in the pan to sear the second side with the pan off the heat); set aside in the skillet.

Heat the remaining 1 tablespoons of olive oil in a large

continued on page 116

serve your community while being
served at Place Pigalle!

visit www.celebratedchefs.com
www.placepigalle-seattle.com

Chef Thomas Schultz

Place Pigalle and the corridors of the world's greatest market at Pike Place are home to Chef Thomas Schultz. Chef Schultz's professional career began, surprisingly, as a sociology student at Gonzaga University. He worked in the hospitality industry to earn money while he earned his degree. After three years working in crisis intervention, Chef Schultz realized his heart belonged back in the restaurant world – and he hasn't turned back.

continued from page 115

skillet over medium-high heat. Add the Brussels sprouts and cook, stirring often, until tender and lightly browned, 4 to 5 minutes. Gently rewarm the beurre blanc over very low heat. Add 3 tablespoons of the pancetta gastrique to the Brussels sprouts and stir to evenly mix (remaining gastrique can be saved for another similar use). Spoon the Brussels sprouts hash onto individual plates and top with the seared scallops. Spoon the prosecco beurre blanc over and serve.

Shellfish

Shellfish remains a subject that puts many cooks on edge, which surely contributes to its popularity on restaurant menus. A few pointers may help make it easier to enjoy cooking shellfish at home.

It's best to purchase shellfish the day you plan to cook them. When you buy clams, mussels and oysters in the shell, you're buying live creatures. If they expire before being cooked, they spoil quickly. To help ensure they're alive, the shells should be very firmly shut, or close firmly when tapped. Discard any with broken or gaping shells. Shellfish need air to survive but should not dry out. Put them in a colander and set inside a larger bowl; top them with damp paper towels and refrigerate. Don't be tempted to submerge in water for storing or cleaning, fresh water will kill them. Clean any shells under cold running water. The tough thread-like "beard" on mussels should be removed just before cooking; grab the beard between your thumb and the back of a knife and tug gently to remove. After cooking, discard any unopened shellfish. It never hurts to buy an extra handful or two of clams and mussels to allow for spoilage.

Scallops are most always shucked when we buy them; so we purchase just the sweet meat with no prep work. Smaller bay scallops come many to the pound. Larger sea scallops can range from basic "large" (an ounce or so each) to huge, weighing a few ounces. Scallops are sold fresh, previously-frozen and still-frozen (sometimes in a re-sealable bag for convenience). In the fresh counter, look for "dry pack" scallops that haven't been treated with chemicals to keep them plump. When buying frozen, choose IQF (individually quick frozen) scallops if you can, for the best quality. Thaw the scallops in the refrigerator overnight to retain a maximum of flavor and rich texture.

Shrimp come in a variety of sizes, both raw and pre-cooked. The smallest "bay" or "cocktail" shrimp are most always precooked and pre-shelled, ready to sprinkle over a salad or toss with cocktail sauce. Medium shrimp are versatile for a range of dishes, and may be precooked or raw. Larger, sometimes called "jumbo" shrimp, are a treat often reserved for elegant appetizers. When you peel the shrimp before cooking, consider popping those shells into a pan of water to simmer for 30 minutes for a quick shrimp stock to be used in a fish soup or add to pasta that has seafood accents. If you can see a dark 'vein' just under the surface of the shrimp's curved back, make a shallow slit with a small knife and lift out the vein. Frozen shrimp can be a great option to have on hand for last-minute dinner options. Select IQF shrimp whenever possible and thaw overnight in the refrigerator.

Because it can be intimidating to cook live Dungeness crab and lobster at home, many seafood markets sell these crustaceans pre-cooked. The clue is the vivid orange color of the shells; both tend to have dark brick- or mahogany-colored shells before cooking. The staff will typically be happy to clean pre-cooked crab for you, which are ready to eat cold or quickly steam to warm through before serving. When a recipe calls for crabmeat, do yourself the favor of buying it in bulk rather than picking your own. Pound-for-pound, it's not much pricier than the amount of meat in a whole crab.

Matt's Rotisserie & Oyster Lounge

Located in the Redmond Town Center, Matt's Rotisserie and Oyster Lounge features global flavors enhanced by a wood–fired grill and rotisserie. Signature techniques, unique ingredients, from scratch recipes, and expert attention to detail provide you with a guarantee of quality and value. Stylish and inviting, the restaurant offers a rich blend of cutting-edge and glowing décor that convey a sense of warmth and comfort.

Grilled Prawns and Scallops with Red Curry Sauce

Kitchen Note: At Matt's they serve the grilled skewers with jasmine rice that's been embellished with fresh ginger and lemon. You'll have extra red curry sauce—which is quite spicy—but it will keep well in the refrigerator for a few days and will be delicious with vegetable or beef stir fry, or simply stirred into steamed rice.

Serves 4

12 large black tiger prawns
8 large sea scallops
8 1-inch squares fresh pineapple
1 tablespoon canola oil
Salt and freshly ground black pepper

Red Curry Sauce

1 tablespoon canola oil
2 tablespoons Thai red curry paste
1 tablespoon finely chopped lemongrass
1 tablespoon packed dark brown sugar
1/4 cup sake
1 can (14 ounces) unsweetened coconut milk
1 kaffir lime leaf or 1/2 teaspoon finely grated lime zest
1 teaspoon Asian fish sauce, more if needed

For the sauce, heat the oil in a medium saucepan over medium heat. Add the curry paste, lemongrass, and brown sugar and cook, stirring, until evenly blended and quite aromatic, 2 to 3 minutes, stirring often. Slowly stir in the sake and cook until reduced and slightly thickened, 2 to 3 minutes, scraping up any cooked bits from the bottom and sides of the pan. Add the coconut milk and lime leaf and bring to a low boil. Reduce the heat to medium-low and simmer until slightly thickened, about 20 minutes. Stir in the fish sauce and taste for seasoning, adding more fish sauce if needed. Set aside.

Preheat an outdoor grill.

Soak 4 8-inch bamboo skewers in cold water for 30 minutes. Drain the skewers and thread 3 prawns, 2 scallops, and 2 pieces of pineapple on each skewer, alternating the items. Brush the skewers with the oil and season lightly with salt and pepper. Grill the skewers until nicely browned on the surface and just a touch of translucence remains in the center, 2 to 3 minutes per side. Gently reheat the red curry sauce (remove the kaffir lime leaf) while the skewers are grilling.

Spoon the curry sauce onto individual plates, top with the grilled skewers, and serve.

Chef Chris Hill

Chef and Partner Chris Matthew Hill's diverse talent features a wide range of scratch recipes and cooking styles from passionate simplicity to inspired innovation. Global flavors are enhanced through the imaginative use of the wood-fired grill and rotisserie. A graduate of the Culinary Institute of America, Chef Hill opened Matt's Rotisserie and Oyster Lounge in 2002 with partner Matt Fleck. He also introduced Hill's Neighborhood Restaurant in Richmond Beach in 2006.

IT'S TIME TO BRING ON THE CENTERPIECE OF THE MEAL

This is the main event. The highlight of your meal. And, thankfully, your options about what to serve are diverse enough to suit every mood and occasion. When you want to wow your friends and family, serve them exquisitely-cooked, tender portions of meats or poultry. Grilled, roasted, fried, stuffed, baked – this portion of the menu is what satisfies the carnivore's dinner dreams.

www.celebratedchefs.com

MEATS AND POULTRY

spring Hill

Spring Hill Restaurant & Bar's emerging chef has a commitment to Northwest foods that are fresh, local, and simple. The wine list boasts a regional focus, and specialty cocktails feature distinctive, house-made flavors. The décor is elegant yet contemporary, with a large display kitchen and soft lighting. Located in West Seattle, Spring Hill is a wholesome new restaurant with an energizing take on food.

Chopper's Red Ale Pork Chop

Kitchen Note: Pork "loin" chops have a similar bone structure to that of T-bone beef steaks. If you are unable to find loin chops, rib chops can be used in their place. Choppers Red Ale from Georgetown Brewery is Chef Fuller's ale of choice for use in this recipe. If you choose to use another red ale, please try to use one that is hoppier than usual. At Spring Hill a common accompaniment to the chops is sautéed mustard greens, potato purée, and apricot jam.

Serves 4

3 bottles (12 ounces each) red ale
1/2 cup packed light brown sugar
1/3 cup kosher salt
1 cup coarsely chopped onion
3 cloves garlic, smashed
2 tablespoons Dijon mustard
3 sprigs fresh thyme
1 bay leaf, preferably fresh
Pinch dried red pepper flakes
4 thick-cut pork loin chops, 10 to 12 ounces each

Combine the ale, brown sugar, salt, onion, garlic, mustard, thyme, bay leaf, and pepper flakes in a large bowl and whisk until the sugar and salt are dissolved.

Add the pork chops to the brine, cover, and refrigerate for up to 8 hours for chops that are 1 1/2 inches or more thick or 6 hours for 1-inch thick chops. If you're using thin chops, 2 to 3 hours will be sufficient.

When ready to cook the chops, preheat an outdoor grill to high heat. Remove the chops from the brine, rinse them lightly, and pat dry with paper towels. Grill the pork chops until nicely browned on the surface and just a hint of pink remains at the center, 4 to 5 minutes per side for thick chops, 2 to 3 minutes per side for thin chops. Set aside, covered with foil, for a few minutes before serving.

serve your community while being
served at spring Hill!
visit www.celebratedchefs.com
www.springhillnorthwest.com

Chef Mark Fuller

Chef and Owner Mark Fuller is responsible for the creativity that is the hallmark of Spring Hill cuisine. Mark, a graduate of the Culinary Institute of America, spent seven years working with Tom Douglas, ultimately serving as Executive Chef at Dahlia Lounge. Chef Fuller, along with wife and business partner Marjorie, opened Spring Hill in the summer of 2008.

Chloé

Chloé Bistrot offers seafood-focused cuisine in an elegant, yet casual French bistro setting. Experience such favorites as "Bouillabaisse de Rascasse," a Provençal seafood stew with saffron and orange zest, or "Crab and Mascarpone Ravioles". Chef Laurent's famous Kobe beef and Brie burger is also showcased on the menu. Nestled in Laurelhurst, dinner at Chloé will feel like you have traveled to Paris just for the evening!

Cuisses de Canard à l'Orange (Duck Legs in Orange Sauce)

Kitchen Note: Depending on the size of the duck legs you are able to find, you may want to serve 2 per person.

Serves 2 to 4

3 navel oranges, preferably organic
2 tablespoons olive oil
4 duck legs, skin removed
Salt and freshly ground black pepper
1 cup white wine vinegar
2 teaspoons sugar
Freshly squeezed juice of 1 lemon

Grate enough zest from the oranges to make 2 tablespoons. Peel all the oranges and cut the flesh into quarters.

Heat the oil in a large skillet over medium heat. Season the duck legs with salt and pepper and brown them well, about 3 minutes per side. Reduce the heat to low, scatter the orange pieces in the skillet, cover, and cook the duck until no longer pink at the bone, 40 to 50 minutes.

Bring a small saucepan of water to a boil. Add the orange zest and cook for 15 seconds, then drain in a fine sieve. Scatter on paper towels to dry.

When the duck legs are fully cooked, transfer them to a plate and cover with foil to keep warm. Add the vinegar and sugar to the skillet and bring to a boil over medium heat, stirring to scrape up cooked bits from the bottom of the skillet. Simmer for 5 to 7 minutes, pressing on the orange pieces with the back of the spoon to extract their juices. Strain the liquid into a small saucepan, pressing on the orange pulp to extract a maximum of flavor. Bring the sauce to a boil and boil to reduce slightly and thicken enough to coat the back of a spoon, 5 to 7 minutes. Stir in the lemon juice and taste the sauce for seasoning adding more salt or pepper to taste.

Arrange the duck breasts on individual plates and drizzle the sauce over. Garnish with the blanched orange zest and serve.

serve your community while being served at Chloé!

visit www.celebratedchefs.com
www.chloebistrot.com

Chef Laurent Gabrel

Chef and Owner Laurent Gabrel was born and raised in Paris, and attended the Cooking School of Versailles. After cooking across the country, Laurent settled in Seattle and opened many restaurants, Chloé Bistrot being his newest. Chef Gabrel is also the owner of Voila! Bistrot in Madison Valley, and at both restaurants, he can often be found in the dining room, greeting customers, pouring wine, or pulling up a seat to chat with friends.

BOKA Kitchen + Bar

BOKA is a vibrant blend of lounge and restaurant. Sleek, contemporary design is infused with a menu of urban American food, award-winning cocktails and New and Old World wines. Chef Angie Roberts sources ingredients that are organically grown, sustainably produced, and purchased from local farmers and producers whenever possible. The seasonal menu is comprised of almost 90% organic ingredients, ensuring the highest quality food available.

Roasted Chicken with Gravy

Kitchen Note: At BOKA this dish is served with flaky, flavorful black pepper biscuits.

Serves 4

4 chicken breasts, skin on, 8 to 10 ounces each
Kosher salt and freshly ground black pepper
2 tablespoons canola oil
2 tablespoons unsalted butter
2 bunches mustard greens, washed, tough ribs
   removed, and leaves coarsely chopped

Gravy

3 tablespoons unsalted butter
3 tablespoons all-purpose flour
2 cups whole milk, more if needed
1 teaspoon apple cider vinegar

Preheat the oven to 450°F.

Season the chicken breasts generously with salt and pepper. Heat the oil in a large ovenproof skillet over medium-high heat until it just begins to smoke. Add the chicken breasts skin side down and cook until lightly browned, 2 to 3 minutes. Add 1 tablespoon of the butter and put the skillet in the oven. Roast until the chicken is no longer pink in the center of the thickest part, 15 to 20 minutes. Remove the chicken from oven and turn the breasts over in the pan. Cover the pan with foil and set aside for 5 minutes.

While the chicken is roasting, make the gravy. Melt the butter in a medium saucepan over medium-low heat. Add the flour and whisk until well incorporated. Cook the flour mixture, whisking often, until it smells warm and nutty but is not starting to brown, 3 to 5 minutes. Slowly whisk in the milk. Increase the temperature to medium

and cook, whisking often, until the mixture begins to thicken. If the gravy becomes too thick, whisk in more milk a bit at a time until you reach the desired consistency. Take the pan from the heat and stir in the vinegar with salt and pepper to taste; keep warm over very low heat.

While the chicken is resting, melt the remaining butter in a large skillet over medium-high heat. Add the mustard greens and cook until they turn a dark green and are just evenly wilted. Season to taste with salt.

Set the chicken breasts on individual plates and spoon the gravy over. Add the greens alongside and serve.

serve your community while being
served at BOKA Kitchen + Bar!
visit www.celebratedchefs.com
www.bokaseattle.com

Chef Angie Roberts

Executive Chef Angie Roberts found herself wearing a chef's toque while studying to be a nutritionist and decided to pursue formal culinary training at Seattle Central Community College. By 21, she was a sous chef at an Italian restaurant in the Market, subsequently working at Earth & Ocean and Flying Fish. At BOKA, she brings a vast knowledge of local produce and grower relationships, and her boundless creativity which evolves with the seasons.

Cellar 46°

Cellar 46° is a neighborhood gathering place where you can sample dozens of wines by the glass, including hard-to-find premium selections, and enjoy casual wine-friendly fare in a warm, inviting atmosphere. Our menu includes offerings such as homemade soups, antipasto plates, fig & chevre crostini, hot crab dip, cedar plank baked salmon, roasted pork loin and pasta, as well as a selection of seasonal desserts.

Flemish Beef Stew

Note: Using a good quality Belgian beer makes all the difference: the richer and darker the better. Potatoes are a perfect partner here, either thick-cut fries or boiled new potatoes.

Serves 6

4 pounds boneless chuck, trimmed and cut into
  2-inch cubes
1 teaspoon salt
1/2 teaspoon freshly ground black pepper
4 to 5 tablespoons all-purpose flour
3 to 4 tablespoons unsalted butter
3 large onions, thinly sliced
24 ounces dark Belgian beer
3 sprigs fresh thyme or 1 teaspoon dried
2 bay leaves, preferably fresh
2 tablespoons Dijon mustard
1 1/2 tablespoons packed dark brown sugar
1 tablespoon cider vinegar or red wine vinegar

Season the beef cubes with the salt and pepper and lightly coat them with flour, patting to remove any excess.

Melt 2 tablespoons of the butter in a large heavy skillet over medium-high heat. When hot, add about 1/4 of the meat and brown well on all sides. Be sure not to crowd the pan so the meat sears well. Brown the remaining meat in batches, adding a bit more butter if needed. As each batch of meat is browned, transfer it to a heavy pot or Dutch oven.

Add 1 tablespoon of the butter to the skillet and melt over medium heat. Add the onions and cook, stirring often, until tender and lightly browned, 15 to 20 minutes. Add the onions to the meat in the stew pot.

Slowly pour the beer into the skillet and deglaze the pan, using a wooden spoon to scrape up cooked bits from the bottom and sides. Bring the beer just to a boil, then pour the liquids over the meat. Add the thyme and bay leaves. Cover and simmer over low heat until the meat is very tender, about 2 hours. Remove the thyme sprigs and bay leaves. Stir in the mustard, brown sugar, and vinegar. If the liquids are quite thin, lift out the meat and set aside; boil the cooking liquids to thicken. Return the meat and the pot and stir gently. Taste the stew for seasoning, adding more salt or pepper to taste. Spoon the stew into individual bowls and serve.

serve your community while being served at Cellar 46°!

visit www.celebratedchefs.com
www.cellar46.com

Chef Nalani Dias

Chef Nalani Dias has long had a passion for cooking. Growing up in Hawaii, she was exposed to a variety of cultures, each with their own distinct culinary flavors and specialties. Some of her most cherished childhood memories include cooking alongside three generations of family for various gatherings. Chef Dias was thrilled to join Cellar 46° and she is pursuing her passion with great success.

Thoa's

Thoa Nguyen is the Seattle chef and restaurateur behind Chinoise Cafe, The Islander, Thoa's and her newest concept, Wabi Sabi Sushi. At Thoa's, diners can savor contemporary Vietnamese cuisine featuring such specialties soft-shell crab summer rolls, seared tuna with rau ram lotus salad and Vietnamese steak frites. Subtle seasonings, fresh herbs, and unique flavors combine to create a memorable dining experience in the heart of Downtown Seattle.

Beef Pho

Kitchen Note: Thai rice sticks are dry flat noodles made with rice flour that are popular throughout Southeast Asia. They come in a variety of widths; a medium size noodle will be ideal here. Look for them with other Asian ingredients in well stocked grocery stores or in an Asian market.

Serves 6

2 1/2 quarts rich beef stock or top-quality canned
   beef broth
3 tablespoons Vietnamese fish sauce, plus more for
   serving
2 cinnamon sticks
4 star anise
1 tablespoon sugar
1 package (13 to 14 ounces) Thai rice sticks
6 green onions
1/2 bunch cilantro, rinsed, dried, and stemmed
1 pound beef sirloin
1 cup loosely packed basil leaves, rinsed and dried
5 limes, quartered
2 jalapeños or 4 serrano chiles, stemmed and thinly
   sliced
1 1/2 cups bean sprouts
Sriracha or other Asian chili sauce, for serving

Put the beef stock in a large stock pot and bring to a boil over high heat. Add the fish sauce, cinnamon sticks, star anise, and sugar, then reduce the heat to medium and simmer while preparing the other pho ingredients.

Bring a large saucepan of water to a boil. Add the rice noodles and cook according to package directions. Drain well and put them in 6 large bowls for serving.

Cut the green onions into thin slices at a deep diagonal. Coarsely chop the cilantro. Cut the beef into the thinnest slices you can, carefully using a sharp knife.

Arrange the basil leaves, lime wedges, and sliced chiles on a platter and set on the table as condiment for the pho when served.

Scatter the bean sprouts, green onion, and cilantro over the noodles in the bowls. Top with the thinly sliced raw beef. Scoop the cinnamon sticks and star anise from the broth and ladle the hot broth into the bowls (the heat of the broth will cook the sliced beef).

Serve right away, passing the condiment platter, Sriracha and fish sauce for guests to add as they wish.

serve your community while being
served at Thoa's!

visit www.celebratedchefs.com
www.thoaseattle.com

Chef Thoa Nguyen

Chef and Owner Thoa Nguyen was born in Vietnam. After Saigon fell, her family moved to Denver, where she grew up and developed her culinary skills by cooking for the family. In 1991, she moved to Seattle, and in 1996 opened the original Chinoise Café on Queen Anne. In 2007, Thoa made her first trip back to Vietnam. While there, she realized she could no longer wait to share her personal interpretations of contemporary and classic Vietnamese dishes with Seattle diners.

Six Seven

Located inside the Edgewater, Seattle's only waterfront hotel, Six Seven offers breathtaking views of Elliott Bay and the Olympic Mountains. Treat your taste buds to inspired, New American cuisine crafted with only the freshest and finest organic and seasonal ingredients. The wine list highlights the finest artisan and boutique bottles from Washington and Oregon wineries along with selections of European and New World vintages, all very well paired to our cuisine.

Herb Brined Chicken

Kitchen Note: A little twist of lemon, and a drizzle of olive oil may be all that is needed to finish this light and juicy main course, which can be served with your favorite vegetables and potato side dish.

Serves 4

1 whole chicken, 3 1/2 to 4 pounds, cut into
  4 portions
1 tablespoon olive oil

Brine

1/2 cup loosely packed fresh flat-leaf parsley leaves
1 stalk celery, chopped
2 shallots, chopped
5 cloves garlic, chopped
3 tablespoons salt
1 tablespoon cracked or coarsely ground
  black pepper
1 tablespoon sugar
1 tablespoon fresh thyme leaves
1 tablespoon rosemary leaves
2 teaspoons fresh tarragon leaves
2 teaspoons fresh oregano
5 fresh sage leaves
Grated zest from 2 lemons
4 cups water

For the chicken, remove the breast, leg and thigh pieces (the entire half chicken) from the carcass without breaking the skin. Complete for each half of the chicken. Once you have separated the chicken pieces from the carcass, remove the thigh bone.

For the brine, combine all ingredients in a high speed blender and puree until smooth (it should taste salty).

Place chicken pieces in a deep dish or bowl and add the brine mixture. The chicken pieces should be fully covered in the brine; add more cold water if needed. Cover the dish and refrigerate to brine for 24 hours.

The next day, preheat oven to 350°F.

Take the chicken pieces from the brine, discarding the brine. Dry the chicken well with paper towels. Now you have 2 half chickens, each with the leg bone in, skin side down. Place the leg and thigh meat over the breast so each half chicken is fully wrapped in its own skin. Lightly oil and salt the top of the chicken and place on an oiled baking sheet or roasting pan. Bake for 15-18 minutes and then remove and rest until it reaches room temperature. To finish, bake chicken at 375°F for 15-20 minutes, or until golden brown. Let sit 5-10 minutes before serving.

serve your community while being
served at Six Seven!

visit www.celebratedchefs.com
www.edgewaterhotel.com

Chef Jordan Mackey

Chef Jordan Mackey brings several years of experience as an Executive Chef to Six Seven, where delicious Northwest cuisine is created in a new light. He prepares local fare with true regional inspiration, using classic techniques to create pure flavors and uncomplicated dishes. The menus at Six Seven are constantly evolving to reflect the harvest and to follow each season's bounty.

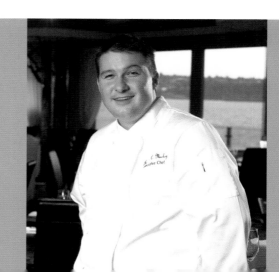

Avila

Every aspect of Avila celebrates craftsmanship, from the delectable food to the comfortable neighborhood atmosphere. Enjoy the amazing diversity and quality of our Northwest bounty, presented with simplicity, elegance and pride. You'll find flavor combinations that delight the senses and draw out the very best from every ingredient.

Lamb in Hay

Kitchen Note: Lamb cooked in hay is a traditional French farmhouse preparation that has become a signature dish of Avila. The hay lends an intense aroma and a different twist on a summer barbeque. It can be hard for urbanites to come by fresh, clean hay. If you are able, certainly use it in this home-style adaptation. Hay or not, the marinated lamb slowly cooked on the grill is delicious even without it; the yogurt will gently tenderize the lamb as it marinates, and gives a pleasant tang to the finished dish. At Avila, the dish is often accompanied by roasted carrots and polenta.

Serves 4

1 1/4 pounds trimmed lamb shoulder or boned leg, trussed with kitchen string
1/4 cup plain whole milk yogurt
3 cloves garlic, finely chopped
2 teaspoons finely chopped fresh marjoram or oregano
1 teaspoon olive oil
2 tablespoons freshly squeezed lemon juice

Stir together the yogurt, garlic, marjoram, and olive oil and rub this mixture all over the lamb. Set the lamb on a plate, cover with plastic wrap, and refrigerate overnight.

The next day, prepare an outdoor grill for indirect heat. If you do have some clean fresh hay, lay a thick bed of it opposite the heat source of the grill. If you have large stalks of herbs from your garden, such as rosemary or bay, you can lay them on the grill instead. Set the lamb on the hay or herb bed, or simply on the grill opposite the heat. Cover and slowly cook until a thermometer reads 135°F when inserted into the thickest part of the meat, 1 to 2 hours. Cooking time will vary with the size and shape of the lamb and the level of heat in the grill; internal temperature is the best indicator to use for doneness.

Transfer the lamb to a cutting board, cover with foil, and let sit for 5 minutes. Cut the lamb into 1-inch slices, removing the kitchen string as you go. Drizzle lemon juice over, sprinkle with salt and pepper, and serve.

serve your community while being served at Avila!

visit www.celebratedchefs.com
www.avilaseattle.com

Chef Alex Pitts

At a young age, Chef Pitts knew he wanted to attend culinary school, and he has now been in the restaurant industry for almost 17 years. During his career, he has worked in many top restaurants across the country. Pitts returned to Seattle in 2007 and worked at Spring Hill prior to the opening of Avila. As Executive Chef, he values his relationships with local farmers, and consistently reflects their offerings in his cooking and seasonal menus.

Dinette

When you step through the doors of Dinette you feel the comfort and intimacy of dining at a friend's home. Dinette features European cuisine that is influenced by the seasons. Simple, soulful, and as inviting as your friend's kitchen, you'll look forward to returning for another evening of memorable, inspired meals, good wine and conversation.

Chile Verde

Serves 6 to 8

3 pounds boneless pork shoulder, cut into
  2-inch chunks
2 teaspoons minced fresh oregano
Kosher salt and freshly ground black pepper
1 pound poblano chiles, roasted and peeled
1/4 cup vegetable oil
1/2 cup all-purpose flour
1 small white onion, thinly sliced
4 cloves garlic, minced
1 tablespoon cumin seed, toasted and ground
1 bottle (12 ounces) Negro Modelo beer
1/4 cup tomato paste
1 pound tomatillos, husked and quartered
2 Anaheim chiles, cored, seeded, and cut into
  2-inch chunks
1 jalapeño, cored, seeded, and minced
1 cup canned green chiles
2 tomatoes, cored and diced
4 cups chicken stock or broth
1/4 cup lightly packed fresh cilantro leaves
1/2 cup sour cream, for serving
Corn tortillas, warmed, for serving

Put the pork pieces in a large bowl and season with the oregano and a couple good pinches each of salt and pepper, tossing well to evenly coat the meat. Cover the bowl and refrigerate overnight.

Roast the poblano chile over a gas flame or under the broiler until the skin blackens, turning occasionally to roast evenly, about 10 minutes total. Put the pepper in a plastic bag, securely seal it, and set aside to cool. When cool enough to handle, peel away and discard the skin. Remove the core and seeds and chop the chile. Set aside.

Heat the vegetable oil in a large pot over medium heat. While the oil is heating, toss the pork pieces in the flour, patting to remove excess. Working in batches, brown the pork well on all sides, 5 to 7 minutes per batch. Set the pork aside in a bowl.

Add the onion to the pot and cook, stirring occasionally, until tender and aromatic, about 5 minutes. Add the garlic and cumin and cook, stirring, for 1 to 2 minutes longer. Stir in the beer and tomato paste and simmer until nearly all of the liquids have evaporated, 8 to 10 minutes. Add the poblano chiles, tomatillos, Anaheim chiles, jalapeño, tomatoes and green chiles. Stir well to blend and cook for 3 minutes. Add the stock and bring just to a boil. Reduce the heat to low and return the pork to the pot, with any accumulated juices. Simmer, covered, until the pork is very tender, about 1 1/2 hours.

Taste the chile verde for seasoning, adding more salt or pepper (or a bit of cayenne for extra heat) to taste. Stir in the cilantro just before ladling the stew into individual bowls. Top each with a dollop of sour cream and serve, passing warm corn tortillas separately.

Chef Melissa Nyffeler

A self-taught chef, Melissa Nyffeler worked as a server before opening a coffee shop. It is here that she discovered a love for cooking and baking, skills honed later at Dahlia Lounge and Le Pichet. Before opening Dinette in 2006, Nyffeler had hosted many family-style dinners at home, which she dubbed "Café Dinette." Chef Nyffeler creates her food "big on flavor and low on pretense" with a stickler's eye for detail.

tidbit bistro

Tidbit is a casual, family-friendly bistro featuring the flavors of Spain and Italy. Presented as main plates and tapas, you can share a nibble of this and that, or enjoy an entrée on your own. Owners John van Deinse and native Italian Nicola Longo believe that natural, fresh ingredients and simple, honest preparation make the best eating. They offer cuisine, wine, and spirits influenced by Madrid and Naples.

Pollo ai Quattro Formaggio

Kitchen Note: Cerignola olives are large, with a firm texture and mild flavor; if you're unable to find them, you can use another type of mild olive. To pit a firm olive such as this, lay the side of a knife blade on top of the olive and press down firmly with your palm. You should then be able to more easily peel the flesh away from the pit.

Serves 4

1 1/2 pounds boneless skinless chicken breast (preferably organic, free range), cut into 3/4-inch cubes
Sea salt and freshly ground black pepper
1/4 cup all-purpose flour
2 tablespoons extra virgin oil, plus more for serving
3 ounces pancetta, finely diced
1 1/2 cups chicken stock or broth
8 Cerignola olives, pitted and halved
3 cloves garlic, minced
2 ounces fresh mozzarella, cut into 1/2-inch cubes
2 ounces fontina, cut into 1/2-inch cubes
2 ounces gorgonzola, cut into 1/2-inch cubes
1 cup loosely packed baby arugula, rinsed and dried
2 ounces Parmigiano Reggiano, shaved into thin slices with a vegetable peeler

Season the chicken pieces evenly with salt and pepper, then toss the chicken in the flour to evenly coat. Pat the chicken pieces to remove excess flour.

Heat the oil in a large skillet over medium heat. Add the pancetta and cook until nicely browned, 2 to 3 minutes. Lift out the pancetta to drain on paper towels. Scoop out all but about 1 tablespoon of the fat from the skillet. Add the chicken pieces and brown well on all side, about 5 minutes total. Reduce the heat to medium, add the garlic, and cook, stirring, for 1 minute. Add the pancetta, stock, and olives and simmer until the chicken pieces are no longer pink in the center, about 5 minutes. Take the skillet from the heat and add the mozzarella, fontina, and gorgonzola cheeses, stirring just to combine. The cheese should melt a bit into the sauce but still hold its shape somewhat.

Spoon the chicken and cheese sauce into individual shallow bowls. Top each with a tuft of the arugula, the shavings of Parmigiano, and a drizzle of olive oil.

serve your community while being served at tidbit bistro!

visit www.celebratedchefs.com
www.tidbitbistro.com

Chef Kurt Stolte

Executive Chef Kurt Stolte became interested in food at a young age watching his mother prepare dinner. Kurt takes a simple approach to food, letting the natural flavor of the ingredients take center stage. He pays close attention to the seasons and focuses on locally grown produce.

Moshi Moshi Sushi

Moshi Moshi brings a unique blend of traditional Japanese cuisine with a contemporary edge to Ballard. When dining, you will be torn between the fresh fish selections in the sushi bar and the cocktail creations in the lounge, both nestled under our mesmerizing LED Sakura tree from Japan. Our menu features fresh seafood from Tsukji Market in Tokyo and top local purveyors. Moshi Moshi is a regular spot for carousers and fine sushi lovers alike!

Shiitake Crusted Steak with Wasabi Cream Sauce

Kitchen Note: White miso paste is available in Asian markets and well-stocked grocery stores. If you're unable to find the white miso, other types of miso paste can be used instead. You can also use a different steak in place of flatiron if you're unable to find that cut; tenderloin and sirloin are two options. Cooking times will vary with the thickness and style of the steak. Blanched asparagus and mashed potatoes will be perfect alongside.

Serves 4

4 flatiron steaks, 6 to 8 ounces each
Sea salt and freshly ground black pepper
1/4 cup white miso paste
6 ounces shiitake mushrooms, wiped clean,
   stemmed, and finely diced

Wasabi Cream Sauce

1 tablespoon unsalted butter
1 tablespoon all-purpose flour
1 cup whole milk
2 tablespoons wasabi paste
1 teaspoon garlic powder
1/2 cup whipping cream
2 teaspoons freshly squeezed lemon juice
Salt to taste

Preheat an outdoor grill.

For the wasabi cream sauce, melt the butter in a medium saucepan over medium heat. Add the flour and cook, whisking, until well blended and frothy, 2 to 3 minutes. Whisk in the milk, wasabi paste, and garlic powder. Bring just to a boil, whisking often, then whisk in the cream. Reduce the heat to medium-low and add the lemon juice with salt to taste. Keep warm over very low heat.

Season the steaks with salt and pepper. Grill until nicely browned on the surface and medium-rare, 2 to 3 minutes per side, longer to suit your taste. Transfer the steaks on a rimmed baking sheet.

Preheat the broiler.

Spread the top of each steak with the miso paste and scatter the diced shiitakes over in an even layer. Broil until mushrooms are lightly browned, 2 to 3 minutes. Remove from broiler and let steaks sit for 5 minutes.

Spoon the wasabi cream sauce onto individual plates and set the steaks on the sauce. Serve right away.

serve your community while being
served at Moshi Moshi Sushi!
visit www.celebratedchefs.com
www.moshiseattle.com

Chef Kevin Erickson

Executive Chef and Owner Kevin Erickson, and his wife Tracy, opened Moshi Moshi Sushi in 2009. Together, they bring a downtown dining experience to their Ballard neighborhood, as well as Bricco della Regina Anna, their Queen Anne spot. Moshi Moshi's contemporary cuisine, coupled with their traditionally trained Japanese sushi chefs, creates an innovative menu with the freshest available ingredients.

The Pike Pub & Brewery

The Pike Pub features traditional pub fare with a special emphasis on local, seasonal, and organic products, with dishes such as crab chowder, wild salmon, hamburgers from grass fed beef, and bratwurst with apple sauerkraut. Pike Ales, brewed on premise in a gravity-flow steam brewery, are featured along with local wines and cocktails using artisan spirits.

Pike Ale Braised Bratwurst with Chef Gary's Apple Sauerkraut

Kitchen Note: The bratwurst used there are made by Uli's Sausages, a neighbor in The Pike Place Market. Look for good sauerkraut sold in bags in the refrigerated section of the grocery store, or from your favorite deli or specialty market. The bratwurst is served at the pub with a healthy serving of horseradish mashed organic potatoes, easy to make by stirring a tablespoon or two of prepared horseradish into your favorite mashed potato recipe. Pike XXXXX Stout Mustard is available at The Pike Pub or you can substitute any high quality stone ground mustard.

Serves 4

2 tablespoons vegetable oil
4 Uli's Kilt Lifter Bratwurst or other top-quality
   bratwurst
1 bottle (12 ounces) Pike Kilt Lifter ale or other
   Scotch style ale
1/2 cup unsalted butter
1 pound yellow onions, diced
1 Granny Smith apple, or any tart-sweet apple,
   halved, cored and chopped
1 tablespoon caraway seeds
1/2 cup packed light brown sugar
1 quart top-quality sauerkraut, well drained
Pike XXXXX Stout mustard, for serving

Heat the oil in a medium skillet over medium heat. Add the bratwurst and brown them well on both sides, 5 to 7 minutes total. Slowly pour the ale into the skillet and simmer over medium-low heat until the sausages are cooked through and most of the liquid has evaporated, about 15 minutes.

While the sausages are simmering, prepare the sauerkraut. Melt the butter in a large skillet over medium heat. Add the onions, apple, and caraway seeds and cook, stirring often, until the onions are tender, about 10 minutes. Stir in the brown sugar then add the sauerkraut and simmer, stirring occasionally, until heated through and the flavors have melded, 10 to 12 minutes.

Transfer the sausages to individual plates (whole, or cut into pieces), spoon the apple sauerkraut alongside, add a spoonful of Pike XXXXX Stout Mustard, and serve.

serve your community while being
served at The Pike Pub & Brewery!

visit www.celebratedchefs.com
www.pikebrewing.com

Chef Gary Marx

Executive Chef Gary Marx has orchestrated the kitchen at The Pike Pub like a symphony conductor since 1997. His love of food, especially spicy soups, sauces, baking, and beer cuisine is evident in the number of accolades The Pike Pub has been awarded through the years.

Portage

Portage restaurant serves French-inspired fare with an influence from the best of the Pacific Northwest region. Tucked away in Upper Queen Anne, you'll find this warm and welcoming dining room, where local, organic ingredients are the starting point of every seasonal menu created by Executive Chef Vuong Loc. Named for his hometown, Portage opened in summer of 2006.

Lamb Chops Stuffed with Carrot Mousse and Dried Cherry Sauce

Kitchen Note: A "Frenched" rack of lamb will have excess fat and bits of meat cut from between the exposed rib bones, making for a tidier presentation. You can ask the butcher to do that for you but have him save you the trim, which will add flavor to the sauce. Caul fat will likely require a special order from your butcher. The thin lacy fat is used by chefs to wrap ground or chopped meats and mousses to hold them together while baking. The fat mostly melts away as it cooks, adding richness at the same time. You'll likely have extra carrot mousse but it would be difficult to make in a smaller quantity; either double the recipe to serve 8, or simply refrigerate the rest to stuff in chicken breasts the next day or simply poach in dumpling form.

Serves 4

1 rack of lamb with 8 ribs, about 1 1/2 pound, Frenched
2 tablespoons olive oil, more if needed
1/2 cup dried cherries
1 shallot, minced
2 cloves garlic, minced
1 teaspoon fresh thyme leaves
1/2 cup dry red wine
1 1/2 cups chicken stock or broth
8 ounces caul fat (optional)

Carrot Mousse

1 cup diced carrot
1/2 pound ground chicken or ground turkey
3/4 cup whipping cream
1 egg
1 tablespoon curry powder
Salt and freshly ground black pepper

For the carrot mousse, bring a small saucepan of salted water to a boil. Add the carrot and simmer over medium heat until very tender, 8 to 10 minutes. Drain well and let cool, then purée the carrot in a food processor until smooth. Add the ground chicken, cream, egg, and curry powder with a good pinch each of salt and pepper. Pulse until well blended, scraping down the sides once or twice. Cook about 1 teaspoon of the mixture in a small skillet until cooked through and taste the sample for seasoning. Add more curry powder, salt, or pepper to the remaining mousse mixture if needed. Transfer to a bowl and refrigerate until fully chilled.

Cut the lamb rack in 4 double-chops and season the pieces well with salt and pepper. Heat the olive oil in a large skillet over medium-high heat. Brown the lamb pieces well on all sides, 3 to 5 minutes total. Set the lamb aside on a plate; reserve the skillet.

For the sauce, to the skillet used to brown the lamb, add the cherries, shallot, garlic, and thyme. Cook over

continued on page 146

serve your community while being
served at Portage!

visit www.celebratedchefs.com
www.portagerestaurant.com

Chef Vuong Loc

Vietnamese-born Chef and Owner Vuong Loc was raised in Portage, Michigan, and later graduated from the Culinary Institute of America in New York. He has cooked extensively throughout the United States, including working for critically acclaimed culinary talents, Charlie Palmer, at Aureole and, Joachim Splichal, at Pinot Brasserie. Chef Loc's approach is classic French - quality ingredients that are carefully handled and beautifully presented.

continued from page 145

medium heat until aromatic and the shallot and garlic
are partly tender, about 1 minute. Add the wine and boil
until reduced by 3/4, 2 to 3 minutes. Add the stock and
boil until reduced by about half, about 3 minutes.
Season to taste with salt and pepper. Set aside.

Optional, if you have some lamb trim, sauté it in 1
teaspoon of olive oil in a small saucepan until lightly
browned, with a bit of chopped carrot, celery, and onion
if you have some on hand. Add the chicken stock and
simmer for 30 minutes, then strain. Add enough water to
make 1 1/2 cups. Use this in place of the chicken stock
above.

Preheat the oven to 450°F.

Set the lamb chops with the curved meaty portion of the
lamb upwards, bone side down. Spoon 3 to 4
tablespoons of the carrot mousse over the meat on each
chop, spreading it neatly to cover the surface of the
chop. If using caul fat, cut it into 4 pieces just large
enough to enclose the chops, wrapping each snugly with
the fat and trimming away excess.

Set the chops on a baking sheet and roast until medium-
rare, 8 to 10 minutes. Let sit for a few minutes before
serving, reheating the sauce gently while the meat rests.

Transfer the lamb chops to individual plates, spoon the
sauce around, and serve.

Romantic Evenings - On the Water

A room with a view. The mere phrase elicits romantic notions of sweeping vistas, mountainous horizons and ruby-hued sunsets. While every restaurant has a distinctive décor based on colors and textures, tableware choices, an ambiance that's established with music and even the staff's attire can be trumped by a setting that makes the surrounding panorama an integral part of the restaurant experience. On those lazy summer evenings or twinkly winter nights, gazing out the window can add a dose of enjoyment to the meal the way a drizzle of aged balsamic vinegar can add finesse to a dish from the kitchen.

In the greater Seattle area, we're lucky to be surrounded by water from many sides, including Puget Sound and Elliott Bay, as well as numerous lakes and other waterways. It allows for ample opportunities to indulge in dinner with a waterfront view.

The Pike Place Market is home to a number of such restaurants, thanks to its perch above Seattle's waterfront. In the Market, you'll find four restaurants that offer distinctive vistas over the historic buildings and produce stalls to catch ferries plying Elliott Bay. And if you time things right, perhaps a kaleidoscope of color as the sun sets over the Olympic Mountains. These destinations include Maximilien (page 112) and Place Pigalle (page 114), which are found to the left and right, respectively, of the beloved butcher Don & Joe's Meats. Across Pike Place, the name of the brick road that dissects the Market, you'll find Chez Shea (page 58) and Matt's in the Market (page 20) upstairs, above the produce stalls of the Sanitary Market building. Through their historic, arched windows, you get a bird's eye view of the Market and its context in the Seattle skyline.

Just south of the Market is ART (page 18) restaurant, in the Four Seasons Hotel. Both the restaurant and lounge area are graced with floor-to-ceiling windows that look out to Elliott Bay and the mountains. For an up-close perspective on the Bay, it's hard to beat Six Seven (page 132) in the Edgewater Hotel, right on the waterfront. This is particularly true from its deck, which sits above the water with a truly sweeping view. From another edge of Elliott Bay, Palisade (page 52) offers waterfront perspective looking out over the Elliott Bay Marina, with the added bonus of views of downtown, and, weather permitting, Mount Rainier in the distance.

For a purely Puget Sound perch, Ray's Boathouse (page 88) has long been a go-to destination to indulge in a distinctly Seattle view, not to mention some great local seafood. Boats pass by on their way through the Hiram S Chittenden Locks, a cruise ship might slip past on its way to Alaska, and those Olympic Mountains add their jagged scrawl to the horizon.

None of these, however, can compete with the view to be had from SkyCity (page 104). Only one restaurant can be found at the 500-foot level of the Space Needle, built for the 1962 World's Fair. During the full 360-degree rotation, diners are treated to a truly eagle-eye perspective on the city, the waterways, hills, neighborhoods and both the Cascade and Olympic mountain ranges.

The Versatility of Pasta and Grains

When it is time to turn to a lighter or meatless main course, you'll find a number of tempting options in the following pages. They're all versatile recipes that could be served in smaller portions as an appetizer, or possibly a side dish to simple grilled beef or pan-seared chicken. In addition, many of these recipes are seasonally flexible. Keep the dish current, like our Celebrated Chefs do, by substituting an "in-season" vegetable or component when the featured ingredient is no longer available.

www.celebratedchefs.com

PASTA AND GRAINS

Palomino

Palomino is open and urban with sleek European lighting, warm colors, blown glass and rich textures throughout. Flavorful and diverse, the cooking style draws influence from Italy, Southern France, Portugal and Spain, all while focusing on local ingredients and seasonality.

Truffle Pea Trenne

Kitchen Note: Trenne is a triangular-shaped short pasta type that is vaguely similar to penne, which can be used in its place. The recipe combines a variety of whatever fresh peas are available, particularly tasty when fresh sweet English peas are in season. No need to worry about truffle season, as the flavor's added to this dish by way of white truffle oil, which is available in specialty food shops and well stocked grocery stores year round. Garlic toast would be an ideal accompaniment.

Serves 2

8 ounces trenne or penne pasta
2 tablespoons olive oil
1 tablespoon minced shallot
1 teaspoon minced garlic
6 ounces mixed fresh peas (shucked English peas, julienned snap and/or snow peas)
2 ounces prosciutto, cut into julienne strips
1 teaspoon finely chopped fresh flat-leaf parsley
1/2 teaspoon finely chopped fresh basil
1/2 teaspoon finely chopped fresh oregano
1/4 teaspoon finely chopped fresh thyme
1 1/2 cups whipping cream
2 tablespoons freshly grated Reggiano Parmigiano, plus thinly shaved for serving
1/2 teaspoon white truffle oil
Sea salt and freshly ground black pepper
2 slices Prosciutto Crisps (see below), broken into large rustic pieces

Prosciutto Crisps

2 large thin slices prosciutto
1 teaspoon olive oil

Bring a large saucepan of salted water to a boil. Add the pasta and boil until al dente, tender but still with a bit of a bite, 10 to 12 minutes.

While the pasta is cooking, heat the olive oil in a medium skillet over medium heat. Add the shallot and garlic and cook, stirring, until tender and aromatic, 1 to 2 minutes. Add the peas and cook until just brightened in color and partly tender, 1 to 2 minutes. Stir in the julienned prosciutto, parsley, basil, oregano, and thyme, then add the cream. Simmer until the cream is reduced by about half, 3 to 5 minutes.

When the pasta is cooked, drain well and add it to the pea sauce with the grated cheese and truffle oil. Toss gently to mix, then taste for seasoning, adding salt and pepper to taste.

For the prosciutto crisps, preheat the oven to 300°F. Line a rimmed baking sheet with a silicone baking mat or parchment paper.

Lightly brush both sides of the prosciutto slices with

continued on page 152

serve your community while being served at Palomino!
visit www.celebratedchefs.com
www.palomino.com

Culinary Director Michael Giampa

Michael Giampa brings over 20 years of culinary and consulting experience to Palomino. Born and raised in Philadelphia, Giampa's love affair with the kitchen began with a childhood tour of a local French restaurant. Today, Michael combines his passion for food with his obsession for local ingredients to create a unique experience at each Palomino restaurant.

continued from page 151

olive oil and lay them in a single layer on the prepared baking sheet. Bake until crisp, 15 to 20 minutes. Set aside to cool.

To serve, spoon the pasta into individual shallow bowls and top with the prosciutto crisp pieces. Scatter shaved Reggiano Parmigiano over the top and serve right away.

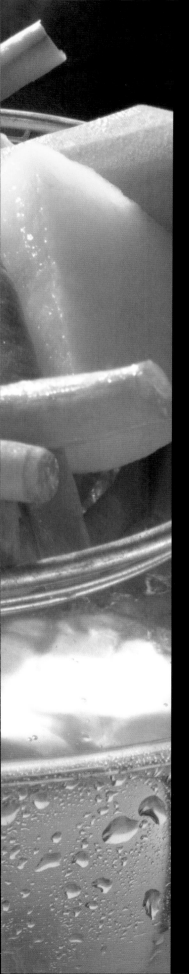

Basic Techniques

Like following the chef's lead on ideal too
easier, arming yourself with some standard
with many recipes in this book, as well as
repertoire. Here are a handful of the basic
Celebrated Chefs in many of these recipe

Toasting nuts:

Before you use them in a recipe develops flavor and
texture. Scatter the nuts in a baking pan and toast
lightly browned and aromatic, gently shaking the pa
nuts, such as pine nuts or slivered almonds, will ne
while whole almonds or hazelnuts many require 10-
helps remove the papery skin from hazelnuts: wrap
towel and let sit for a few minutes, then rub the tow

Peeling tomatoes:

Can seem like a tedious chore until you learn an ea
small "X" in the bottom of each tomato and gently a
water. When you see the skin start to split, which ca
to 30 seconds, depending on type and ripeness, lift
and plunge it into a bowl of ice water. This helps st
tomato becoming too soft. When cooled, just peel a
fingers and proceed as directed. The same techniq
peaches.

Clarifying butter:

Is used by chefs in instances where they want the f
knack for burning and becoming bitter. Clarifying th
solids, leaving pure butter fat that can withstand hi
clarify butter, melt it slowly over low heat in a small
skim away any foam from the surface, then pour the
the solids behind in the bottom of the pan.

Blanching and refreshing:

Is a classic chef's technique used when preparing
involves adding them to a pot of boiling water to co
depending on the recipe). Then they are quickly dr
bowl of ice water. This important step quickly cools
cooking and set the color. Once chilled, you can the
before using as needed in the recipe.

Segmenting oranges:

Cleanly is necessary when a chef wishes to remove
membrane from each segment, leaving just the juic
cut both ends from the fruit, just to the point that th
the fruit sitting upright on the cutting board, cut dov
of the skin, carefully following the curve of the fruit.
bowl to catch the juice and segments—slip the blad
membrane and flesh of each segment to remove it.

Tavolàta

By definition, Tavolàta means to gather around the table, and that is exactly what you'll find - people gathered around the tables and bar - at this vibrant Italian eatery in Seattle's Belltown neighborhood. The large communal table, running the length of the industrial room, is ideal for sharing bowls of house-made pasta, creative Italian dishes and toasting simple pleasures with friends.

Bigoli with Garlic, Chili, and Anchovy

Kitchen Note: This dish exemplifies the beauty of simplicity. While you could substitute spaghetti in the recipe; thick, whole wheat bigoli has such a wonderful flavor and texture that you should give it a try at least once. Bigoli, similar to bucatini, is an extruded pasta like spaghetti but the center is hollow. Don't be put off by the amount of anchovy called for; the fish melt into the oil and add an incredible depth of flavor.

Serves 4

1 pound bigoli pasta, preferably whole wheat
3 cloves garlic, sliced
2 teaspoons dried red pepper flakes
12 oil-packed anchovy fillets, drained and chopped
3/4 cup olive oil
1/4 cup chopped fresh flat-leaf parsley

Fried Breadcrumbs

1/4 cup olive oil
2 cloves garlic, crushed
8 ounces bread slices, stale or lightly toasted,
  broken into pieces
Kosher salt

For the fried breadcrumbs, combine the oil and garlic in a small saucepan over medium-low heat. When the oil is warm, set the pan aside to infuse for about 10 minutes. Meanwhile, pulse the bread in a food processor to make fine crumbs. Add the crumbs to the garlic oil and cook over low heat until the crumbs are toasted and have absorbed the oil, 2 to 3 minutes. Season to taste with salt. Set aside about 1/3 cup of the crumbs; extra will keep in an airtight container for about 2 weeks.

Bring a large pot of salted water to a boil. Add the pasta and cook for 1 minute less than is recommended in package instructions.

While the pasta is cooking, heat the olive oil in a large sauté pan over medium-low heat. Add the anchovy, garlic, and pepper flakes. Cook gently, stirring occasionally and poking at the fish fillets, until the garlic is tender and the anchovies melt into the oil.

When the pasta is done, drain it well and add it to the sauté pan. Add the parsley and toss well. Divide the bigoli between 4 deep bowls and top each with a generous tablespoon of the fried breadcrumbs. Serve immediately.

serve your community while being
served at Tavolàta!

visit www.celebratedchefs.com
www.ethanstowellrestaurants.com

Chef Ethan Stowell

Ethan Stowell is a self-trained natural in the kitchen who finds his inspiration in fresh ingredients and clean flavors. He has received many accolades, including being named one of the *2008 Best New Chefs in America* by *Food & Wine* magazine. As the chef and owner of four highly acclaimed restaurants, Ethan is deeply committed to seeing that Seattle, his hometown, is nationally recognized as a top culinary destination. His first cookbook, *Ethan Stowell's New Italian Kitchen*, is available this fall.

Piatti

Rustic, flavorful cuisine and simple, unpretentious designs recreate the warmth and charm of a traditional Italian trattoria at Piatti Ristorante & Bar. Reminiscent of a restaurant in Tuscany, the restaurant is a gathering place where friends, family, and neighbors eat, drink, and socialize. The open kitchen and stone pizza hearth delight diners with a seasonally driven menu and extensive wine list of Northwest & Italian wines.

Rigatoni with House-made Fennel Sausage, Tomato and Pecorino Romano

Kitchen Note: At Piatti, they grind their own pork shoulder to use for this sausage meat. If possible, ask your butcher to grind you some good quality pork to order. A mini-processor will be a great tool for chopping the pancetta; dice the pancetta first, then pulse off and on in the processor until it has about the same texture as the ground pork. Alternatively, look for a good quality bulk Italian-style sausage, adding 1/2 teaspoon or so of fennel seeds to the mixture.

Serves 6 to 8

1 pound dried rigatoni
2 tablespoons olive oil
1 pound homemade fennel sausage or good
  quality Italian sausage
1/2 teaspoon dried red pepper flakes, more to taste
1 can (28 ounces) peeled whole plum tomatoes,
  drained and chopped into small pieces, liquid
  reserved
1/2 cup chopped flat-leaf parsley
1/4 cup dry white wine
4 ounces Pecorino Romano, grated

House-made Fennel Sausage

1 pound ground pork, preferably freshly ground
2 ounces pancetta, finely ground or finely chopped
2 teaspoons kosher salt
2 teaspoons dried oregano
2 teaspoons chopped garlic
1 teaspoon fennel seeds, lightly chopped
1/2 teaspoon crushed or coarsely ground black
  peppercorns
1/4 teaspoon cayenne pepper

Bring a large pan of salted water to a boil. Add the rigatoni and cook until partly tender but still a bit firm, about 8 minutes (2 minutes less than package instructions). Scoop out and reserve about 1/2 cup of the pasta cooking liquid, then drain the pasta, discarding the rest of the water. Return the pasta to the pan and set aside.

Heat the olive oil in a large skillet over medium heat. Add the sausage and cook until evenly browned, 8 to 10 minutes, breaking it up into small pieces as it cooks. Add the pepper flakes and cook for about 30 seconds, stirring. Add the tomatoes, reserved tomato liquid, and parsley and cook, stirring occasionally, until the mixture thickens slightly, 10 to 12 minutes, stirring occasionally. Stir in the wine and cook for 1 to 2 minutes longer.

Add the sauce and the reserved 1/2 cup pasta water to the rigatoni. Cook, stirring gently, for about 3 minutes so the water is almost completely absorbed and the pasta is tender and picks up a reddish color. Stir in all but 1/4 cup of the cheese.

continued on page 158

*serve your community while being
served at Piatti!*

visit www.celebratedchefs.com
www.piatti.com

Chef Felix Acosta

Executive Chef Acosta was exposed to the industry at a very young age. His father was a baker, his mother worked at an ice-cream-cone factory, and he spent summers at his uncle's supermarket. After trying a few careers, Chef Acosta enrolled in culinary school. He spent several years cooking in many of Seattle's finest restaurants before joining Piatti as Executive Chef in August of 2002.

continued from page 157

To serve, spoon the rigatoni and sauce into shallow pasta bowls, sprinkling the reserved cheese over.

For the Piatti's house-made fennel sausage, combine the pork, pancetta, salt, oregano, garlic, fennel seeds, black pepper, and cayenne pepper in a large bowl. Stir well to evenly mix.

Comfort Cooking - Back to Basics

You can say that the economy's driving our interest in comfort foods lately. But really, when is there not a time that it's nice to dig your spoon into a bowl of something that makes you feel as though all is right with the world?

Chefs realize how much attachment we have to perennial comfort-food favorites. No matter how up-scale their restaurant may be, you often will see familiar favorites listed on the menu. Just don't be surprised if the dish you're served isn't exactly as you remembered it! That "mud pie" on the dessert list may not be the mile-high version you relished when you were younger. Instead you'll likely see that the chef has created a revamped version of the beloved dessert, still appealing to our emotional connection to foods that comfort us. It can be both new and familiar at the same time.

Macaroni and cheese, hot dogs, grilled cheese, fried chicken, pot pie—there are dozens of ways that comfort foods are manifested on today's menus. And of course, everyone's idea of comfort food is different! For someone from Switzerland that might be cheese fondue, while for someone with Vietnamese heritage, it could be a steaming bowl of phô. Comfort food is often tied to childhood memories of meals that made us feel cozy, loved, and safe. The recipe pudding could be peppered with raisins and vanilla bean in one person's comfort-food memories, while to another it's scented with saffron and rose water. That can be part of the fun!

Expand your comfort food repertoire by sampling dishes that reflect those same strong emotional ties for diners from a culture different from your own. Comfort comes in a range of delicious styles! And it may be a bit less home-style when you're dining out, but chefs still echo the warmth and familiarity with their creative interpretations of our comfort food favorites.

Monsoon East

Award-winning Monsoon East, located on Bellevue's historic and independent Main Street, highlights Vietnamese cuisine with local, organic, free-range ingredients from the Pacific Northwest. The restaurant offers a chic, casual setting and the menu is complemented by a full bar and creative wine list. Experience the restaurant's Ocean Bar; fresh, local oysters and fluke sashimi with fried shallots are just a few of the items you will enjoy.

Dungeness Crab Congee with Chanterelle Mushrooms and Ginger Relish

Kitchen Note: If you can't find chanterelle mushrooms substitute another type of wild mushroom such as black trumpet, morel, or hedgehog. The better the stock you begin with, the more delicious this congee will be; it's a good time to make a batch of homemade chicken stock.

Serves 6

2 quarts chicken stock or broth
3 tablespoons peanut oil
3/4 cup long grain rice
1 1/2 cups coarsely chopped chanterelle
    mushrooms, about 6 ounces
Kosher salt and freshly ground black pepper
12 ounces Dungeness crab meat
1 tablespoon chopped fresh cilantro

Ginger Relish

3 tablespoons minced fresh ginger
2 tablespoons extra virgin olive oil
2 tablespoons freshly squeezed lime juice
1 tablespoon minced shallot
1 teaspoon minced chives

Combine the chicken stock and 2 tablespoons of the peanut oil in a large saucepan and bring to a boil. Stir in the rice, reduce the heat to medium-low and cook, stirring occasionally, until the mixture is thick and creamy, about 1 1/2 hours.

While the congee is cooking, preheat the oven to 400°F. Toss the mushrooms with the remaining 1 tablespoon of the peanut oil. Scatter the mushrooms on a baking sheet and roast until tender and lightly browned, 8 to 10 minutes.

For the ginger relish, stir together the ginger, olive oil, lime juice, shallot, and chives. Season to taste with salt and pepper.

Taste the congee for seasoning, adding salt if needed. Ladle the congee into individual shallow bowls. Add the crabmeat to the center of each bowl, spooning the roasted mushrooms to one side of the crab and the relish to the other side. Top the crab with chopped cilantro and a grinding of black pepper. Serve right away.

serve your community while being
served at Monsoon East!

visit www.celebratedchefs.com
www.monsooneast.com

Chef Nathan Crave

Originally from upstate New York, Executive Chef Nathan Crave moved to the Pacific Northwest as a teenager. After graduating from the Culinary Arts Program at North Seattle Community College, Nathan spent time working under many celebrated chefs in both Seattle and Boston. Today, Crave enjoys the challenge, set forth by owners Eric and Sophie Banh, of cooking modern Vietnamese cuisine, while infusing Pacific Northwest flavors and his own innovative style.

sazerac

Sazerac provides the perfect backdrop for a uniquely seductive food concept, where the motto is "Serious Fun and Damn Good Food." This stylish downtown Seattle destination provides a high-ceilinged room, elevated exhibition kitchen and vibrantly designed interior, featuring whimsical chandeliers in rich colors of amber and red. At Sazerac you'll find eclectic private rooms, innovative cocktails, and a phenomenal happy hour.

Ricotta Dumplings with Sweet Corn and Pancetta

Kitchen Note: The pancetta used here should be in roughly 1/4-inch thick slices, as it will be diced and sautéed. If you're not able to request it custom-cut at the deli counter, you can use thick-cut bacon instead.

Serves 4

1/2 cup diced pancetta, about 3 ounces
1 tablespoon unsalted butter
1 cup freshly cut sweet corn kernels
1 clove garlic, minced
1 1/2 cups halved cherry tomatoes
Salt and freshly ground black pepper
Shaved Parmesan cheese, for serving

Ricotta Dumplings

1 1/2 cups whole milk ricotta cheese
2 egg yolks
1 1/4 cups all-purpose flour, more if needed
3/4 cup freshly grated Parmesan cheese
1/4 teaspoon salt
Pinch freshly ground black pepper
Pinch freshly grated or ground nutmeg
1 tablespoon olive oil

For the dumplings, combine the ricotta cheese and egg yolks in a large bowl and stir to evenly blend. Combine the flour, cheese, salt, pepper, and nutmeg in a medium bowl and stir to mix. Add the dry ingredients to the ricotta and stir just until fully and evenly incorporated. Transfer the dough to a lightly floured work surface and knead lightly until cohesive, 2 to 3 minutes, adding a bit more flour if needed. Form the dough into a ball, wrap in plastic, and let sit at room temperature for 30 minutes.

Divide the dough into 4 even pieces. Roll 1 piece of the dough into a rope of 1/2-inch diameter, keeping the remaining dough covered. Cut across the rope into about 1 1/4-inch pieces to form the dumplings. You can roll the pieces on a grooved gnocchi board (if you have one) to create the traditional ridged surface.

Bring a large pan of salted water to a boil over high heat. Reduce the heat to medium-high and add half of the gnocchi. Cook until the gnocchi float to the surface, 2 to 3 minutes. Lift the dumplings from the water with a slotted spoon and drain on paper towels. Repeat to cook the remaining gnocchi, allowing the water to reheat as needed. Put the gnocchi in a large bowl and toss with the olive oil; set aside.

Warm a sauté pan over medium high heat, melt butter, add dumplings and allow to brown slightly. Add pancetta, garlic and corn and sauté for a minute or two just warm fresh ingredients through. At the last moment add tomatoes. Season with salt and pepper.

To serve, place in a shallow pasta bowl, sprinkle with the shaved Parmesan, enjoy.

serve your community while being served at sazerac!

visit www.celebratedchefs.com
www.sazeracrestaurant.com

Chef Jason McClure

Executive Chef Jason McClure has been at the helm of the Sazerac culinary team since its inception in 1997. He believes in "food being fresh, simple and focused." After graduating with a degree in Hospitality Management from Northern Arizona University, McClure cooked his way across the country. With a knack for blending the South's soul-soothing tastes with the flavors from the Pacific Northwest, McClure gives Sazerac its singular essence.

Ristorante Italianissimo

Ristorante Italianissimo has been Woodinville's outpost for fine dining since 1996. Every component of their classical Northern Italian cuisine is prepared from scratch. Fresh seafood and meats are brought in on a daily basis and local produce is used whenever possible. The extensive wine list features a composition of Italy's best, as well as wines from Washington and California.

Penne with Prosciutto and Gorgonzola Cream Sauce

Kitchen Note: This pasta can also be served as a side dish to roasted or braised meats, such as chicken, pork, or beef.

Serves 2

8 ounces penne pasta
2 tablespoons unsalted butter
3 ounces prosciutto, diced
3/4 cup whipping cream
2 ounces gorgonzola, crumbled
Salt and freshly ground black pepper
Freshly grated Parmesan cheese, for serving
Coarsely chopped flat-leaf parsley, for serving

Bring a large saucepan of salted water to a boil. Add the pasta and boil until tender but still with a bit of a bite, about 10 minutes. Drain well and set aside.

Melt the butter in a large skillet over medium-high heat. Add the prosciutto and cook, stirring often, for 1 to 2 minutes. Add the cream and cook, stirring, to bring the cream just to a boil. Stir in the gorgonzola with salt and pepper to taste. Simmer to reduce slightly and thicken the sauce a bit, 2 to 3 minutes. Add the pasta to the sauce and stir to evenly coat in the sauce and reheat the pasta.

Spoon the pasta and sauce into shallow pasta bowls or plates. Scatter Parmesan cheese and parsley over and serve right away.

serve your community while being served at Ristorante Italianissimo!

visit www.celebratedchefs.com
www.italianissimoristorante.com

Chef Kent Betts

With a regionally famous restaurateur as a mother, Chef Kent Betts has had the culinary lifestyle ingrained in him since his preteens. He worked his way through high school and college in his family's restaurants, then spent a dozen years cooking at restaurants along the West Coast. Chef Betts purchased Italianissimo in 1996 and has been cooking every day since.

Firenze

Since 1992, Firenze has been serving homemade recipes to diners who quickly become regulars. Italian conversations mingle amid opera music, while the aroma of delicious Italian fare stirs the senses. Whether you are planning a romantic dinner, toasting a business deal, or celebrating with family, Firenze is the perfect place to relax and enjoy outstanding Italian cooking and the finest Italian wines.

Spaghetti Aragosta

Serves 2

2 tablespoons extra virgin olive oil
2 Maine lobster tails, in the shell, about 6 ounces
    each, halved lengthwise
1/4 cup finely chopped red onion
1 tablespoon minced garlic
1 tablespoon chopped fresh flat-leaf parsley
1 large pinch Spanish saffron
6 ounces canned San Marzano tomato sauce
1/4 cup whipping cream
Salt and freshly ground black pepper
12 ounces spaghetti
8 baby arugula leaves, for serving

Bring a large pot of salted water to a boil. Add the spaghetti and cook until al dente, tender but still with a bit of a bite, 10 to 12 minutes.

While the pasta is cooking, prepare the sauce. Heat the olive oil in a large sauté pan or deep skillet over medium-high heat. Add the lobster tails, onion, garlic, parsley, and saffron. Cook, stirring often, until the onion is tender and lightly browned, 2 to 3 minutes. Add the tomato sauce and cream, reduce the heat to medium-low and cook, stirring occasionally, until the sauce is thickened a bit and the lobster is opaque through the thickest part, 6 to 8 minutes. Season to taste with salt and pepper.

Drain the pasta well and add it to the sauce. Toss well to evenly coat, then arrange the pasta and sauce on individual plates, laying the lobster tails on top. Garnish with arugula leaves and serve.

serve your community while being
served at Firenze!

visit www.celebratedchefs.com
www.firenzerestaurant.com

Chefs Rosendo Ruiz and Salvatore Lembo

Chef and Owner Salvatore Lembo grew up in Italy and prides himself on serving authentic Northern Italian cuisine with a personal touch. Executive Chef Rosendo Ruiz has proudly been cooking at Firenze for over 17 years. Together, Lembo and Ruiz craft a seasonal menu that reflects the time honored, family recipes of Lembo's heritage. In traditional Italian fashion, guests are greeted like old friends and Ruiz's authentic cooking is always memborable.

And Now for a Sweet Finale

A sweet finale. To many, a meal's not complete without a sweet conclusion. It is the true finishing touch to a satisfying dining experience. For these diners, the dessert list is often the first part of the menu to peruse and provides early guidance to the perfunctory selections that precede it.

The following pages contain tempting ideas that are certain to finish your dinner party on a high note. Whether you're looking for a comfort-food classic, or the occasion calls for a touch of panache, you'll find several delectable options. The decision either to "tease" your guests with the knowledge of the dessert that will provide the finale to your meal, or to keep it a secret, is up to you.

www.celebratedchefs.com

DESSERT

Boat Street Café

A Provençal sensibility inspires both food and space at the Boat Street Café. You'll eat the simple, sturdy, luscious food of French grandmothers, made of the freshest ingredients, mostly from local farmers. The room with its slate tables, mismatched chairs, and warm oak floors, is bathed in the amiable glow of candlelight and cream-colored walls.

Vanilla Bean Rice Pudding with Blackberry Compote

Serves 4 to 6

1 1/2 cups whipping cream
2 cups whole milk
3/4 cups arborio rice
1/4 teaspoon salt
1 vanilla bean, halved lengthwise
1/3 cup sugar
Blackberry Compote

Blackberry Compote

1 pound fresh or frozen blackberries
1 cup sugar
3/4 cup dry red wine
1 tablespoon freshly squeezed lemon juice
1 teaspoon finely grated lemon zest
1 small sprig fresh rosemary
Pinch salt

Combine the cream, 1 1/2 cups of the milk, rice, and salt in a medium saucepan. Use the tip of a small knife to scrape the tiny seeds from the halved vanilla bean. Add the vanilla seeds and the bean halves to the cream mixture, stirring well to mix. Bring just to a boil over medium-high heat, stirring occasionally, then reduce the heat to low and cook until the rice is tender and the mixture is thick and creamy, 20 to 25 minutes. Take the pan from the heat and stir in the sugar and the remaining 1/2 cup of the whole milk. Lift the vanilla bean halves from the mixture, running your fingers down the length of the beans to extract a maximum of flavor.

For the blackberry compote, combine the berries, sugar, wine, lemon juice, lemon zest, rosemary, and salt in a small heavy saucepan. Bring just to a boil over medium-high heat, then reduce the heat to medium-low and simmer until thickened and aromatic, about 20 minutes. Transfer to a bowl and let cool; remove the rosemary before serving.

Serve warm, or chilled. Either way, spoon the blackberry compote over the rice pudding just before serving.

serve your community while being served at Boat Street Café!
visit www.celebratedchefs.com
www.boatstreetcafe.com

Chef Renee Erickson

Chef Erickson has been involved in cooking and art since age 22. While earning an art degree, she also worked at the then, fledgling Boat Street Café. After a traveling and eating stint in Europe, she entered into the food fray as the young new owner of, none other than Boat Street Café. Her commitment to fresh, local, foraged and farmed, preferably organic ingredients, continues to expand. Renee lives in Ballard with her dog Jeffry, cat Lucca and a potager.

Lark

Welcome to Lark, a rustic neighborhood restaurant located in Capitol Hill. Local artisans, farmers and foragers contribute to an ever-changing menu that offers the best of each season — bright and intense with summer, heartening and rich in the fall. Small plate courses of cheese, charcuterie, vegetables, grains, fish, and meats inspire communal dining with waves of flavors arriving at your table.

Mission Fig Tarte Tatin with Chèvre Sorbet

Kitchen Note: You may have some of the puff pastry sheet left over; bake topped with cinnamon sugar or grate Parmesan for a quick snack.

Serves 6

1 sheet puff pastry, thawed if frozen
6 large black mission figs, just ripe, or 12 dried whole figs or apricots
1 egg, lightly beaten
Powdered sugar, for serving

Caramel Sauce

1 cup sugar
1/4 cup corn syrup
1/4 cup water
3 tablespoons unsalted butter, cubed
1/2 cup whipping cream
2 tablespoons grappa, rum, or brandy
Pinch salt

Chèvre sorbet

1 cup water
1 cup sugar
1 cup whipping cream
1 cup chèvre (fresh goat cheese)
1 tablespoon freshly squeezed lemon juice
1/2 teaspoon salt

For the caramel sauce, combine the sugar, corn syrup, and water in a small, heavy saucepan over medium heat. Stir until the sugar is fully dissolved, then stop stirring while it cooks to a deep amber caramel color, 10 to 12 minutes. You can gently swirl the pan to help assure the sugar cooks evenly but avoid stirring. Take the pan from the heat and add the butter a bit at a time, whisking gently to blend it with the caramel as it melts. Gradually whisk in the cream then add the grappa and salt. When the caramel is well blended, set aside to cool. Transfer to a bowl and refrigerate until needed.

Preheat the oven to 400°F. Line a baking sheet with a silicone baking mat or parchment paper. Cut 6 3-inch squares from the puff pastry sheet.

Spoon 1 teaspoon of the caramel in 6 spots equally spaced on the baking sheet. Cut each fig into about 1/4-inch slices, keeping the slices attached at the stem end if possible. Fan 1 fresh fig or 2 plumped dried figs over each dollop of caramel. Top each portion of figs with a square of puff pastry and brush the pastry lightly with the beaten egg. Bake until the pastry is browned and puffed, 12 to 14 minutes.

For the chèvre sorbet, combine the water and sugar in a small saucepan and bring just to a boil over medium heat, stirring to help the sugar dissolve. Boil for 2 minutes, then set aside to cool completely.

continued on page 174

serve your community while being served at Lark!
visit www.celebratedchefs.com
www.larkseattle.com

Chef John Sundstrom

A graduate of the New England Culinary Institute, Chef John Sundstrom came to Seattle in 1991, where he cooked in such restaurants as Dahlia Lounge, Carmelita and Earth & Ocean. He opened Lark with his wife, JM Enos, and partner Kelly Ronan, in December 2003. Sundstrom has received many national accolades, including the *James Beard Foundation* award for *Best Chef Northwest/Hawaii* in 2007.

continued from page 173

Combine the cooled syrup, cream, chèvre, lemon juice, and salt in a medium bowl and whisk until smooth. Refrigerate until fully chilled then freeze in an ice cream maker according to manufacturer's instructions. Transfer to a plastic container and freeze for at least 4 hours before serving.

To serve, let the tarte tatins cool for a few minutes on the baking sheet, then transfer them, inverted, to individual plates. Drizzle more of the caramel sauce around and add a scoop of sorbet alongside. Sprinkle powdered sugar over all and serve.

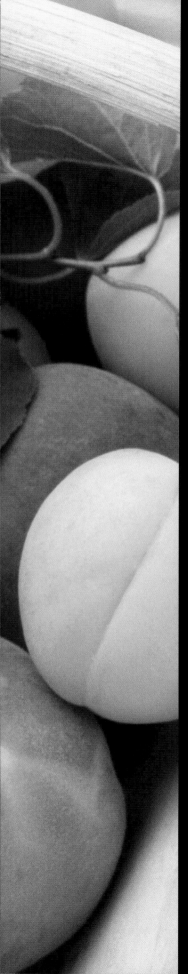

Washington Fruits

There is a great array of foods that claim a spot in the lineup of outstanding regional Northwest products: salmon, wild mushrooms, asparagus, hazelnuts, oysters, farmstead cheese, the list is long. It's easy to get enthusiastic about all these delicious items that make their way to our dinner plates in Seattle.

And when it comes to dessert? We're not doing too badly in that department either. Apples quickly come to mind; it is the official state fruit after all, and longtime #1 agriculture product of Washington. Additionally, the state ranks as the top producer of apples in the country and has for many years. The annual match-up between rivals University of Washington and Washington State University is dubbed the Apple Cup in honor of its stature.

A new crop of locally-harvested apples is a sure sign of fall in the Seattle area which means that woolen sweaters, chill foggy mornings, and kitchen windows steaming up from pots of warming soup can't be too far behind. Pears, too, though a much smaller production, are an equally-welcome autumn treat.

But apples aren't the only star fruit in Washington. Others for which the state leads production nationally include red raspberries, sweet cherries and plums. And there are a number of fruits for which Washington ranks in the top five producers in the United States, including apricots, blueberries, peaches, strawberries, and cranberries. It's a near embarrassment of riches.

Stone fruits are among the most luscious of those grown in the region. This is the family of juicy, soft fruits that have a pit: apricots, cherries, plums, nectarines and peaches. Peach pie, cherry crumble, a delicate little apricot tart. Simple preparations such as these showcase those fruits beautifully.

And who doesn't love berries? The jewel-toned fruits of summer brighten up everything they touch, whether it's a morning bowl of granola or a classy crème brûlée after dinner. Local burger joints throw them into their milkshakes, and countless cobblers are made for backyard barbecues. Berries add bright, sweet flavor and plenty of color to our lives.

To be fair, the state's fruits are certainly not just for dessert! Sweet cherries make their way into savory salsas and chutneys that are delicious with grilled or braised meats. Berries are added to vibrant salads, maybe with a sprinkling of fresh goat cheese or rings of sweet onion. Plums or apricots sautéed with chicken or lamb echo Middle Eastern traditions of cooking meats and fruits together. Or how about chilled nectarine soup with a scattering of freshly snipped basil to start a summertime dinner? These outstanding fruits are delightfully versatile and add great flavor and texture to the menus of the Northwest.

Trellis

Trellis' menu evolves with the seasons, always using the best of the harvest as a foundation. Dishes are inspired by what Chef Brian Scheehser grows on his ten-acre farm in Woodinville. From the fruit and vegetables gathered daily (or pulled from cold storage in the winter) to livestock and seafood from local artisan producers, your dining experience will truly celebrate the bounty of the Pacific Northwest.

Lemon Sage Flan

Serves 8

2 teaspoons unflavored gelatin powder
   (1 envelope)
1/4 cup cold water
2 cups whipping cream
2/3 cup whole milk
1/2 cup sugar
3 tablespoons freshly squeezed lemon juice
2 teaspoons freshly grated lemon zest

Sage Syrup

1/2 cup water
1/2 cup sugar
4 sage leaves, plus more for garnish
Candied lemon zest, for garnish

Sprinkle the gelatin over the water in a small dish and let it soften for 5 minutes.

Combine the cream, milk, sugar, and lemon zest and juice in a saucepan over medium heat. Heat, whisking occasionally to help the sugar dissolve, until wisps of steam rise but not to the point of boiling, about 5 minutes. Take the pan from the heat and add the softened gelatin, whisking gently until fully dissolved. Pour the mixture into lightly oiled espresso cups or other small dishes. Let cool completely, then cover with plastic wrap and refrigerate until fully set, at least 2 hours or overnight.

For the sage sauce, combining the water, sugar, and sage leaves in a medium saucepan over medium heat. Warm the mixture, stirring occasionally until sugar is dissolved, 2 to 3 minutes. Simmer gently until aromatic and slightly thickened, 2 to 3 minutes, then set aside until cooled. Strain the sauce and refrigerate until ready to serve.

Just before serving, run a thin knife around the outer edge of each panna cotta and unmold them into the center of a shallow soup bowls. Spoon the sage syrup around and garnish with the candied lemon zest and sage leaves.

serve your community while being served at Trellis!

visit www.celebratedchefs.com
www.heathmankirkland.com/trellis

Chef Brian Scheehser

At Trellis, Chef Scheehser blends modern cooking techniques and flavor profiles with the rustic farm-fresh robust cooking style characteristic of wine country restaurants. Committed to sustainable farming, Scheehser lays a table of food and drink that uses fresh, regional ingredients at the height of their seasonality. Trained at the Culinary Institute of America, Chef Scheehser has over 30 years of culinary experience.

spur Gastropub

Spur nods to the area's pioneer fishermen and occasional outlaw roots, with its iconic and historic American imagery. Diners find interactive and seasonally pure plates, where sustainably conscious dishes feature farm-to-table, native ingredients. Signature items include pork belly sliders, seasonal rotations like pan-seared trout, and daily chalkboard menus. Cocktail pairings and desserts are an additional vibrant cornerstone to Spur.

Microwaved Chocolate Sponge Cake

Kitchen Note: This dessert is deceivingly simple. A siphon, available at nicer cooking stores and most commonly known as a whipped cream dispenser, is the secret to this effortless cake. Chefs McCracken and Tough suggest finishing this decadent dessert with a scoop of your favorite chocolate gelato or ice cream.

Serves 1

3 egg whites
1 egg yolk
1 ounce milk chocolate
2 ounces dark chocolate
1/2 cup granulated sugar
1/2 cup Canola Oil
1/2 Cup Cake or Pastry Flour
Pinch of salt

Place chocolate in microwave safe bowl. Melt chocolate in microwave for 1 1/2 minutes, or until fully melted. Meanwhile, place eggs, sugar, oil, and salt into a blender, and blend for 30 seconds. Add melted chocolate, and blend for another 30 seconds. Pour into mixing bowl, and then whisk sifted flour into mixture. Immediately pour into 1 pint sized whipped cream siphon. Screw on lid, add 1 nitrogen cartridge. Shake and let sit for 30 minutes at room temperature. Fill an 8 ounce paper cup half full with batter, and microwave on high for 40 seconds. Let sit for one minute, and serve immediately with a scoop of gelato or ice cream.

serve your community while being
served at spur Gastropub!
visit www.celebratedchefs.com
www.spurseattle.com

Chefs Brian McCracken and Dana Tough

Schooled in techniques from around the world, Chefs and Co-owners Brian McCracken and Dana Tough showcase New American cuisine, where sustainably conscious dishes feature farm-to-table native ingredients. McCracken comes from a family of fishermen and farmers and has studied with some of the nation's top chefs. Tough, the former Chef de Cuisine at Tilth restaurant, is most inspired by his local farmers' crops.

Betty

Located at the top of Queen Anne Hill, Betty Restaurant & Bar opened in 2007. The sister restaurant to Crow Restaurant, Betty has a slightly calmer atmosphere with it's mellow blue walls and dark wooden booths. Betty offers guests the perfect atmosphere for a relaxing dinner. Similarities between the two restaurants are their Chef's Counters and the comforting, seasonal foods served without pretense or fuss, at prices that are easy to swallow.

Seville Orange Flan

Kitchen Note: Seville is a type of orange that is quite bitter, too much so to eat as fresh fruit but ideal for making marmalade. The distinctive character of the Seville orange adds wonderful flavor to this rich flan, though blood oranges or navel oranges can be used instead.

Serves 6

3 cups whole milk
Freshly grated zest of 1 large (or 2 small)
  Seville oranges
2 vanilla beans, split lengthwise
4 whole eggs
7 egg yolks
3/4 cup sugar
Pinch of salt
1 tablespoon Grand Marnier or other orange flavored liqueur

Caramel

1 1/2 cups sugar
1/3 cup water

Combine the milk and orange zest in a medium saucepan. Run the tip of a small knife down the length of each vanilla bean half to remove the tiny seeds. Add the seeds and the beans to the milk. Bring just to a boil over medium-high heat, then take the pan from the heat, cover, and let steep for 2 hours.

Preheat the oven to 325°F. Lightly oil 6 6-ounce ramekins and set them in a roasting pan that is lined with a kitchen towel (this keeps the ramekins from sliding around).

For the caramel, combine the sugar and water in a small, heavy saucepan. Stir very gently with a wooden spoon until the sugar is dissolved. Set the pan over high heat and cook, brushing down the sides of the pan now and then with a pastry brush lightly moistened with water. Once the sugar reaches an nice amber color, take the pan from the heat. Carefully pour the caramel into the ramekins to evenly coat the bottoms. Set aside while making the custard.

Whisk together the whole eggs, egg yolks, sugar, and salt in a large bowl. Take the lid from the pan with the milk and bring it just to a boil again. Whisking constantly, gradually add the warm milk to the egg mixture. Continue whisking gently until the sugar is fully dissolved. Strain the custard into a medium bowl and stir in liqueur.

Pour the custard into the prepared ramekins. Half-fill the roasting pan with very hot water and cover it with foil. Bake until the flans are set, no longer jiggly in the center, 1 to 1 1/4 hour.

continued on page 182

serve your community while being served at Betty!

visit www.celebratedchefs.com
www.eatatbetty.com

Chef Brittany Bardeleben

Pastry Chef, Brittany Bardeleben developed her passion for baking during childhood, and fondly remembers Mom's Rhubarb Dump Cakes and Grandma "Mamo's" Blackberry pies. She graduated from culinary school in 2000, and has since, baked in many kitchens and operated a wholesale bakery. Brittany joined Betty when it opened in 2007, where she found a home for her clean, straightforward approach to desserts, and her grandmother's pie recipes!

continued from page 181

Take the pan from the oven and let cool until the ramekins are cool enough to handle. Lift them from the water bath and let cool to room temperature. Cover the ramekins with plastic wrap and refrigerate overnight.

Just before serving, run the tip of a small knife around the outer edge of each flan. Set a dessert plate upside down on top of a ramekin and carefully flip both together to unmold the flan onto the plate. Lift the ramekin slowly, so that the caramel drips down over the flan. Repeat with the remaining flans and serve.

Tea

What's old is new again. How many times has that applied to the trend of the day, whether cocktails (I'll have a Manhattan, please!), fashion, film, or food. In the case of tea - which is enjoying a surge in popularity lately - it's more appropriately "what's ancient is new again." Tea leaves have been steeped to make a bracing beverage for many centuries, and today, has something of a new allure that is re-introducing many people to it's pleasures.

It used to be that when you ordered a cup of tea in a restaurant, you would likely receive a cup, a little pot of hot water, and one lonely tea bag sitting on the saucer. Perhaps, to be fair, you did have a choice to make: regular or herbal. Today the choices, and the presentations, are given greater care, as more and more restaurants are devoting as much attention to the beverages they serve as they do the dishes that come from the kitchen.

Part of the growth of interest in tea can be attributed to its health benefits, coupled with increasingly open trade channels from Asia that bring more and more varied supplies into the country. Beyond that, more and more consumers are learning about the extensive array of types of tea, finding that there is something for everyone, from the deepest rich Assam black tea to a calming rooibos-hibiscus-mint blend.

Though we often think of tea and coffee as cohorts in the hot beverage realm, it has been said that tea is more like wine than coffee. From one single plant, Camellia sinensis, all black, green, oolong, and white teas are made. The same leaves and buds harvested at different times and processed in different ways result in a wonderfully diverse realm of teas to explore.

Add to that the category of herbal teas, and the world of tea selections increases dramatically. Beyond the more familiar chamomile and mint selections, today, you may see rooibos teas, made from the needles of a South America bush that create a no-caffeine beverage with rich flavor and mahogany-red color (sometimes known as "red tea"). Or yerba mate from South America, an herbal tea that has the surprising quality of being high in caffeine, said to offer the stimulation of coffee without its subsequent crash.

There are many tea companies based in the Northwest, from well known brands such as Stash and Tazo, to smaller, newer companies that include Smith Tea and Tao of Tea in Portland, and Remedy Teas and Barnes & Watson in Seattle. "T" from Vancouver and Mighty Leaf and Numi from California are also select brands served in many local restaurants. Tea has become so popular in the region that Seattle is now home to the annual Northwest Tea Festival, held the first weekend of October. And would you believe that there's even tea now being grown in the Northwest? Though popular wisdom would suggest that the region's climate isn't too friendly to the heat-loving Camellia sinensis, a couple local farmers have been dabbling in growing tea. So don't be too surprised when one day, the restaurant server asks if you might like a nice Skagit Valley blend to enjoy after dinner.

Madison Park Café

Owner Karen Binder originally opened Madison Park Café as a coffee and tea room in 1979. The Café has grown into the quintessential neighborhood restaurant, serving some of Seattle's finest French bistro dinners. You can enjoy this fare outside in the cobblestone courtyard or indoors by the glow of the fireplace. Emphasis is on locally grown and sustainable, seasonal food prepared with a French flair.

Vanilla Bean Crème Brûlée

Serves 4

4 egg yolks
1 1/2 cups whipping cream
3 tablespoons sugar, plus more for caramelizing
1 vanilla bean, split lengthwise
Fresh berries, for serving (optional)

Preheat the oven to 325°F.

Whisk together the whole egg and egg yolks in a medium bowl. Set aside.

Combine the cream and sugar in a medium saucepan. Use the tip of a small knife to scrape the tiny seeds from the halved vanilla beans. Add the vanilla seeds and the beans to the cream. Scald the cream over medium heat, whisking occasionally to help the sugar dissolve. Try to avoid allowing the cream to come to a full boil.

Slowly add about 1/2 cup of the warm cream to the egg mixture, whisking constantly until fully blended. Gradually add the remaining cream, whisking constantly. Strain the custard mixture into a lipped measuring cup, discarding the vanilla bean halves.

Set 4 crème brûlée dishes or 4-ounce ramekins in a large baking dish. Pour the custard into the dishes, to about 1/8 inch from the top. Carefully pour hot water into the baking dish to come about halfway up the sides of the crème brûlée dishes. Cover the baking dish snuggly with foil and bake until the custards are set, 25 to 35 minutes (timing will vary with the type and size of dishes used).

Remove the foil and let the custard cool until easy enough to handle, then transfer the dishes to a wire rack to cool completely. Refrigerate until well chilled, at least 2 hours or overnight.

Just before serving, take the custards from the refrigerator. Sprinkle a thin, even layer of sugar (about 1 teaspoon) over each custard. Use a kitchen blow torch to caramelize the sugar to a rich medium brown. Let cool for a few moments, then serve, topped with fresh berries if you like.

serve your community while being
served at Madison Park Café!

visit www.celebratedchefs.com
www.madisonparkcafe.ypguides.net

Chef Rich Coffey

Beginning as the pastry chef, Rich Coffey quickly became the Executive Chef at the Madison Park Café. Previously he worked at Campagne, Au Bouchon French Bistro, Cafe Septième and the Sorrento Hotel, bringing 20 years of cooking and pastry experience to the helm of the Madison Park Café. Chef Coffey takes pride in offering the classic French dishes that he loves, with a twist to make them unique.

Ventana

Ventana Restaurant invites you to experience Chef Joseph Conrad's contemporary twists on American favorites, with a focus on small plates, seasonally inspired dishes, and family-style dining. Through floor-to-ceiling windows, the view here competes only with the foods for admiration. Join us for our twice daily happy hour seven days a week!

Fennel Ice Cream

Kitchen Note: You'll need about 1/2 of a medium fennel bulb roasted for this recipe. You can either roast just that half, saving the rest for fresh use, or roast the whole thing and use the extra tossed into a pasta dish or sliced to add to a salad.

Makes 1 1/2 quarts

1 medium fennel bulb
2 1/2 cups whole milk
2 1/2 cups heavy cream
1 tablespoon fennel seeds, toasted
8 egg yolks
1 cup sugar

Preheat the oven to 400°F.

Trim the fennel bulb, reserving the tender green fronds. Halve the fennel lengthwise and cut out the tough core. Wrap the fennel bulb in a piece of foil and roast until very tender, about 45 minutes. Set aside to cool. Chop the fennel bulb; 1/2 cup is needed for the ice cream. Chop enough of the fennel fronds to make 1 tablespoon.

Combine the milk, cream, and fennel seeds in a medium saucepan and warm over medium heat for 10 minutes. Whisk the egg yolks in a large bowl and add the sugar, whisking until well blended and the color lightens a bit. Slowly add about 1 cup of the warm milk to the egg yolks, whisking constantly. Slowly whisk this into the saucepan and cook over medium-low heat until thick enough to coat the back of a spoon, 5 to 7 minutes. Set aside to cool slightly.

Put the fennel bulb in a blender and pulse a few times to finely chop it. Add the fennel fronds and about half of the ice cream base. Purée until very smooth, about 1 minute. Put this in a large bowl with the remaining ice cream base and refrigerate until fully chilled. When properly chilled, churn the ice cream according to your machine's instructions. Transfer the ice cream to a plastic container and freeze until ready to serve.

serve your community while being served at Ventana!

visit www.celebratedchefs.com
www.ventanaseattle.com

Chefs Joseph Conrad

Originally from Des Moines, IA, Chef Joseph Conrad is a graduate of the California Culinary Academy. Joseph earned his chops, training at Chicago's prestigious Charlie Trotter restaurant and later honed his skills in some of San Francisco's finest kitchens (Aqua, Rubicon and 415). In 2007, Chef Conrad moved to the Northwest and served as chef at Qube. He later joined the Twist team and led the opening of its restaurant sibling, Ventana, in 2009.

Library Bistro & Bookstore Bar

Reminiscent of a 1940s and 1950s style restaurant with high back booths, 10-foot high bookcases, and copper and bronze checkerboard tiles, Library Bistro provides a cozy neighborhood feel while serving contemporary American food. The award-winning seasonal menu packages with the color and inspiration of impressionist masterpieces, while other works of art line the shelves and walls.

Meyer Lemon & Rosemary Cake

Kitchen Note: Two wonderfully aromatic ingredients combine in this simple cake. When Meyer lemons are unavailable, regular lemons are an ideal substitute.

Serves 8

3/4 cup granulated sugar
2/3 cup olive oil
5 egg yolks
1/2 cup whole milk
Finely grated zest and juice from 3 Meyer lemons
4 teaspoons finely chopped fresh rosemary
1 teaspoon pure vanilla extract
1 2/3 cups all-purpose flour
2 teaspoons baking powder
1/4 teaspoon salt
Rosemary sprig for garnish

Icing

1 1/2 cups powdered sugar, sifted
1/4 cup freshly squeezed Meyer lemon juice

Preheat the oven to 350°F. Butter a 9- by 5-inch loaf pan and dust it with flour, tapping to remove excess. Cut a piece of parchment paper about 4 inches wide and 15 inches long to line the length of the pan and come up the sides by an inch or so.

Beat together the oil and sugar until well blended, with a whisk or in a stand mixer. Add the egg yolks one at a time, beating well after each addition. Add the milk, lemon zest and juice, rosemary, and vanilla and whisk gently until well blended.

Sift together the flour, baking powder, and salt into a small bowl or onto a piece of waxed paper. Gradually whisk these dry ingredients into the batter, careful not to overmix. Pour the batter into the prepared loaf pan and bake until a toothpick inserted in the center comes out clean, 40 to 45 minutes. Let cool slightly on a wire rack, then turn the cake out onto a cutting board.

For the icing, stir together the powdered sugar and lemon juice. Slice the cake and arrange them overlapping on a serving platter. Drizzle with the icing and serve, with a sprig of rosemary for garnish if you like.

serve your community while being
served at Library Bistro & Bookstore Bar!
visit www.celebratedchefs.com
www.librarybistro.com

Chef Tiffany Layco

Chef Tiffany Layco discovered her passion for cooking when a job as a server took her into the kitchen. She never left. Giving up the pursuit of a medical degree, she set her sites on the Western Culinary Institute, then several exclusive West Coast restaurants before joining Library Bistro as Executive Chef. Chef Layco holds an appreciation for French and Japanese cooking, as well as a love for Latin, South East Asian and Italian flavors.

The Georgian

The ultimate Seattle fine-dining experience, guests at The Georgian enjoy seasonal menus that reflect local flavor and ingredients. Whether it is a romantic dinner for two, a power lunch, or classic Georgian tea, be treated to warm, engaging service, against the backdrop of a beautiful dining room.

Oreo Mud Pie

Kitchen Note: To get the finest cookie crumbs for coating these spheres of ice cream, use a food processor and pulse frequently until fine crumbs are formed.

Serves 6

1 pint top-quality vanilla ice cream
1 pint top-quality coffee ice cream
1 cup finely ground Oreo or other chocolate
   wafer crumbs
Caramel Sauce (see below)
Chocolate Sauce (see below)

Caramel Sauce

1 1/4 cups sugar
3 tablespoons water
1/4 teaspoon freshly squeezed lemon juice
1 tablespoon light corn syrup
3/4 cup whipping cream
2 tablespoons unsalted butter

Chocolate Sauce

1 cup water
3/4 cup sugar
1/4 cup light corn syrup
1/2 cup unsweetened cocoa powder
8 ounces bittersweet chocolate, chopped

Set both ice creams in the refrigerator to soften gently, just to the point that you can easily scoop the ice cream but it still firmly holds its shape. Put the Oreo crumbs in a shallow dish.

Scoop up about 2 tablespoons of the vanilla ice cream and 2 tablespoons of the coffee ice cream and work quickly to form them together into a ball. Roll the ice cream in the cookie crumbs to evenly coat, then set on a rimmed baking sheet and freeze while making the rest. When all the ice cream has been formed, cover the pan with plastic wrap and freeze until fully firm, about 1 hour.

For the caramel sauce, combine the sugar, water, and lemon juice in a medium, heavy saucepan and bring just to a boil over medium-high heat, stirring to help the sugar dissolve. Stir in the corn syrup and cook, without stirring, until the mixture reaches a deep amber caramel color, 6 to 8 minutes. Slowly, carefully add the cream, whisking gently to blend with the caramel and form a smooth sauce. Take the pan from the heat and whisk in the butter. Set aside to cool.

For the chocolate sauce, combine the water, sugar, and corn syrup in a medium saucepan and bring just to a boil over medium-high heat, stirring to help the sugar dissolve. Take the pan from the heat.

continued on page 192

serve your community while being
served at The Georgian!

visit www.celebratedchefs.com
www.fairmont.com/seattle

Chef Artis Kalsons

Executive Pastry Chef, Artis Kalsons, has more than 20 years of culinary experience, bringing expertise, enthusiasm, and creativity to his work. A native of Riga, Latvia, Kalsons knew as a young boy, that pastry was his passion. Kalsons attended culinary school at age 16 and after his second year, he began interning in many kitchens. Today, Kalsons oversees and leads the entire pastry kitchen at The Fairmont Olympic and its restaurants.

continued from page 191

Put the cocoa powder in a medium bowl and gradually whisk in just enough of the sugar syrup to form a smooth paste. Whisk for a few moments to blend well, then gradually whisk in the remaining syrup. Melt the chocolate in the top of a double boiler or in the microwave, stirring until smooth. Add the melted chocolate to the syrup mixture and whisk until smooth.

Spoon the caramel and chocolate sauces onto one side of individual plates, arrange the ice cream balls alongside, and serve.

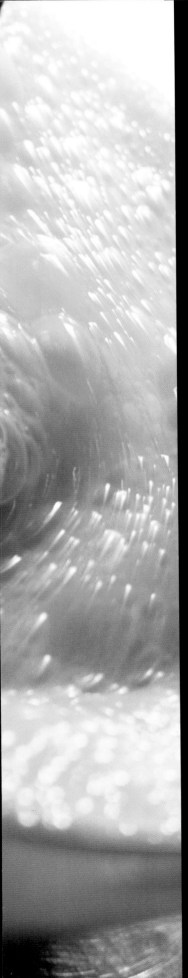

Modern Cooking

Some call it molecular gastronomy, others prefer to think of it simply as a modernist's approach to cooking. Whatever name it takes, you've likely seen some interesting new things on your dinner plates when eating out recently. Foams of Parmesan cheese or gelled formations of herb purées, sous vide-cooked salmon* or freeze-dried strawberries.

It might seem a bit over-the-top, but there really is more than just novelty at play in many of today's top kitchens. This new wave of cooking exemplifies the fact that part of what drives many who make a career of cooking is the constant adventure and exploration that they can enjoy, working with new foods and new techniques. It's not all that different than mini-burgers taking countless kitchens by storm, chefs playing their own riff on the trend and having fun while they do so. Or kumquat having its moment in the spotlight as the "it" fruit and working its way into a range of dishes as chefs experiment with their own creative impulses.

Where modern cooking transcends the status as a culinary trend is that it is so widely applied in today's kitchens, across a range of types of dishes. It's not simply about sous vide or foams, instead it references a broader discipline that is generally looking at cooking through fresh, creative eyes. And yes, there is a lot of science at play. But when you think about it, science is pretty much always at play in the kitchen! Marinating meat to infuse flavor and tenderize. Whipping egg yolks with oil to emulsify into mayonnaise. Beating egg whites with a bit of sugar to create a glossy foam of meringue. Modernist chefs simply expand on those timeless themes in exciting new ways, expressing innovative approaches to food in delicious ways.

Some of the tools for modern cooking are surprisingly easy to come by. In fact you can technically cook something sous vide in a pot on your stove, it just requires some extra-careful monitoring of heat levels for accurate cooking. And foams can be dispensed from the same type of re-usable canister that is often used to make whipped cream (though today's chefs might add an extra ingredient to help stabilize the foam, so it doesn't dissipate right away). Other modern methods do require very specialized ovens or other pieces of equipment that aren't practical for most home kitchens.

In these pages you may see a bit of foam on an occasional recipe, but we opted to not expect your home kitchens to have an NO^2 canister on hand. So we typically have amended the garnish on those dishes to use, say, slivered fresh basil instead of basil foam. You'll have that thoroughly modern dining experience with the luscious foam and other accoutrements of contemporary cooking, when you dine out at these marvelous restaurants.

Sous vide, meaning "under vacuum", is a French cooking method where fresh ingredients are cooked in vacuum-sealed plastic bags in hot water. The food maintains maximum flavor because it is slow-cooked for an extensive period of time at a relatively low temperature.

Queen City Grill

Located north of the Pike Place Market in the heart of Belltown, the Queen City Grill reigns as one of the area's favorite dining spots. For over two decades, the restaurant has wooed urbanites with cocktails, grilled fresh fish, and a comfortable, see and be seen atmosphere. They specialize in simply cooked Northwest seafood, locally grown organic produce, and an award-winning 500 label wine list.

Fresh Apple Pie Drizzled with Caramel

Kitchen Note: If you do not have a favorite recipe, try Fran's Classic Caramel (or any other high-quality dessert sauce as a substitution).

Serves 8

6 large apples, about 3 pounds, cored, peeled, and sliced
1/3 cup sugar, plus more for pastry
2 teaspoons cornstarch
1 teaspoon ground cinnamon
Pinch ground cloves
Pinch freshly grated or ground nutmeg
Pinch salt
1 egg, lightly beaten (optional)
Caramel Sauce for serving

Pastry Dough

3 cups all purpose flour
1 1/2 tablespoons sugar
1 1/2 teaspoons finely grated orange zest
1 teaspoon salt
1 1/2 cups unsalted butter, cut into pieces and chilled
1 teaspoon pure vanilla extract
1/2 cup ice water

Put the flour in a food processor with the sugar, orange zest, and salt. Pulse a few times to blend. Add the butter pieces and pulse just until the mixture has the texture of coarse cornmeal. Add the vanilla and pulse once, then add about 1/4 cup of the water, pulsing a few times to blend. Add just enough of the rest of the water to form a smooth dough that's not sticky. Turn the dough out onto the work surface and form it into 2 even disks. Wrap them in plastic and refrigerate for at least 30 minutes. Roll 1 portion of the dough out on a lightly floured work surface to a round about 14 inches across. Use this round to line a 10-inch pie pan.

Put the apples in a large bowl. Toss together the sugar, cornstarch, cinnamon, cloves, nutmeg, and salt in a small bowl and stir to mix. Add the spice mixture to the apples and toss to evenly mix. Fill the pie shell with the apples, mounding slightly in the center.

Roll out the remaining portion of dough on a lightly floured work surface to a round about 12 inches across. Top the apple filling with the pastry round and trim both the bottom and top pastry edges with a slight overhang. Pinch the edges together with your fingers to form a well-sealed and decorative edge. Make a few slits in the top dough to allow steam to escape during baking. For a sugary topping to the pie, brush the dough with the beaten egg and sprinkle lightly with sugar.

Bake the pie at 350°F until the pastry is well browned and the apples are tender when pierced through one of the slits in the top of the pastry, about 1 hour 15 minutes. Set aside to cool on a wire rack.

Cut into generous wedges, transfer to plates and drizzle caramel sauce along side and serve.

serve your community while being served at Queen City Grill!

visit www.celebratedchefs.com
www.queencitygrill.com

Chef Oscar Montejano

Executive Chef Oscar Montejano has been with Queen City Grill for nearly 10 years. Raised in San Francisco, Oscar has had a long culinary history working in many top rated restaurants in the Bay Area and Seattle. Chef Montejano brings a unique Spanish flair to his cooking style and infuses it in his creations. He always looks to local, organic sources in preparing his seasonal menu, while offering a little spice and sophistication to every dish.

Dulces Latin Bistro

Take the bounty of the Pacific Northwest, fuse it with the glory of French, Spanish and Italian cooking, add a dose of Mexican flair, and you get the Euro-Latin cuisine of Julie Ann Guerrero. Co-owner Carlos Kainz, whose 32 years in the business is fueled by his passion for wine, has an expansive 1,200 bottle wine list. The duo proudly knows most guests by name and what they like, and attribute this personal attention to Dulces' success.

Strawberry Coconut Cream Tart

Serves 8

1 cup whipping cream
1/2 can (about 3/4 cup) unsweetened coconut milk
1/4 cup shredded coconut
1/4 teaspoon pure vanilla extract
1/2 cup sugar
1/4 cup cornstarch
1 whole egg
2 egg yolks
10 to 12 large fresh strawberries, hulled and thinly
    sliced

Sweet Pastry Dough

1 1/2 cups all-purpose flour
1/2 cup unsalted butter, cut into cubes and chilled
1/4 cup sugar
1/4 teaspoon salt
1/8 teaspoon baking soda
1 egg white
2 to 3 tablespoons ice water

For the pastry dough, combine the flour, butter, sugar, salt, and baking soda in a food processor and pulse until well blended and the mixture has the texture of coarse sand. Add the egg white and pulse to thoroughly blend. Drizzle in enough cold water to just form a cohesive dough. Turn the dough out into the work surface and form it into a disk; wrap well in plastic and refrigerate for at least 1 hour or overnight.

Preheat the oven to 375°F.

Cut the dough into 8 even piece and roll each out to a circle about 7 inches in diameter. Use the pastry rounds to line 4-inch tartlets pans, preferably with removable bases. Line each tartlet shell with a piece of parchment paper and add pie weights or dry beans to fill the shells. Bake the shells until lightly browned and set, 12 to 15 minutes. Lift out the paper and cook a few minutes longer to ensure the pastry is fully and evenly cooked. Set aside to cool completely.

Combine 1/4 cup of the sugar with the cornstarch, whole egg, and egg yolks in a medium bowl and whisk well to blend. Set aside.

Combine the cream, coconut milk, remaining 1/4 cup sugar, coconut, and vanilla in a medium saucepan. Bring just to a boil over medium-high heat, whisking to blend and help the sugar dissolve. Gradually add about 1/2 cup of the warm liquid to the egg mixture, whisking constantly. Gradually whisk this back into the pan with the remaining liquids and cook over medium heat, whisking occasionally, until thickened, 3 to 4 minutes. Transfer to a bowl, lay a piece of plastic wrap directly on

continued on page 198

serve your community while being
served at Dulces Latin Bistro!
visit www.celebratedchefs.com
www.dulceslatinbistro.com

Chef Julie Ann Guerrero

Executive Chef and Co-Owner Julie Guerrero has her own unique style of cooking. Her Latin menu (defined by the fusion of French, Spanish, Italian) and regional Mexican flavors changes seasonally to take advantage of the freshest Pacific Northwest ingredients available. Born and raised here, Guerrero is a South Seattle Community College culinary school grad. Her exceptional desserts explain why the restaurant takes the Spanish name for "sweets."

continued from page 197

the surface of the custard, and set aside to cool to room temperature. Refrigerate until fully chilled, about 30 minutes. Remove the tartlets from their tins and set the shells on individual plates. Spoon the coconut filling into the prepared tartlet shells, smoothing the surface. Top each tartlet with slices of strawberry, overlapping them slightly. Serve right away.

Mise en Place

One of the very best lessons we home cooks can take from professional chefs is that of "mise en place". It's a French term (which translates roughly as "putting in place") for the basic principle of getting all your ingredients and tools prepped and organized before you begin a recipe.

Be sure to read the recipe all the way through—both ingredients and method—before you start so there won't be any surprises. In fact, it's a good idea to do so at least a day ahead if you can, in case you need to budget time for marinating meat or for a dessert that needs to chill overnight before it is served.

First, look closely at the ingredient list. It's not a matter of just having your carrots, tomatoes, hunk of cheese, and head of lettuce on hand. Part of the goal with mise en place is to do any advance preparation needed before you begin step one of the recipe. You don't want to have to stop midway through because you hadn't noticed that the butter should be at room temperature or nuts need to be toasted. Check what kind of prep each ingredient needs and take care of that first. Be sure your herbs and onions are chopped, lettuce greens rinsed and dried, cheese grated, mushrooms wiped clean, and so on.

Beyond simply streamlining the cooking process, "mise en place" can also help you parse out some of the cooking time so you don't have to tackle the whole thing in one fell swoop. Grated cheese, roasted garlic, toasted nuts, these and many types of prep can be done a day or two in advance, rather than having to do all the prep and cooking at the same time. Not all ingredients are quite so flexible though. More delicate items like grated citrus zest and chopped lettuce should be done shortly before they're needed.

The more you cook at home, the more you should consider investing in a variety of small dishes, great to have on hand for organizing all this glorious prep work you will have done. Ramekins of a few different sizes, mini gratin dishes, small nested bowls, they'll all come in handy. Then once you launch into the first step of the recipe method, you'll feel just like one of those television chefs or cooking school teachers, the ones who look so polished and don't have to break momentum once they get started. When you get in the groove of doing your mise en place, you may be surprised how much more comfortable and easy the whole cooking process ends up being.

94 stewart

Chef owned and operated, 94 Stewart is a Northwest style bistro fashioned to seamlessly meld into the historic surroundings of Pike Place Market. Offering fresh seafood and local farm-raised meats, guests can feel at home in their favorite attire while dining on world-class food and wine. Their service provides the perfect combination of professionalism and friendliness, ready to answer any question about the area, food, and wine.